Connected

Connected

Curing the Pandemic of Everyone Feeling Alone Together

ERIN DAVIS

B&H
PUBLISHING GROUP
Nashville, Tennessee

978-1-4336-8258-2

Published by B&H Publishing Group
Nashville, Tennessee

Dewey Decimal Classification: 248.843
Subject Heading: WOMEN \ LONELINESS \ SOLITUDE

1 2 3 4 5 6 7 • 18 17 16 15 14

To my twin sister, Nikki.
God knew I would wrestle with loneliness.
I'm so thankful He's given me a friend since the womb.

Contents

CHAPTER 1

The Seismic Shift

It was an epic moment. A star took the stage in a beautiful, designer gown and accepted a prestigious award. In a sea of people with eyes fixed squarely on her, she was not alone. Perhaps that's why our mouths collectively fell open when she looked into the cameras and made this confession.

"I want to be seen, to be understood deeply and to not be so very lonely."[1]

You might recognize that line as part of Jodie Foster's acceptance speech for the Cecil B. DeMille lifetime achievement award at the 2013 Golden Globes. It was a speech that left many scratching their heads. How is it possible for someone so famous to be lonely? Why did her lonely confession cause so many of us to squirm? Are we a society uncomfortable with loneliness? If so, is that because loneliness is unfamiliar to us or because we know the sting of loneliness a little too well?

I've never won a lifetime achievement award. My designer is Target (preferably off the clearance rack) and my wedding was the last time I squeezed into anything that could be described as a "gown." I'm not famous and have never felt the burn of the white-hot spotlight . . .

But I know what it's like to be lonely.

It all started with a seismic shift.

The Seismic Shift

My calendar was jam-packed with things to do, people to see, and activities to attend. My e-mail in-box was full of correspondence from friends and acquaintances. Some days my phone never stopped ringing. If you had asked me to name my friends, I could have hammered out a long list. By all appearances I seemed well connected.

Loneliness Lesson #1: Appearances can be deceiving.

My husband, Jason, had been on staff at a church for twelve years. That meant that for our entire marriage and most of my adult life we were hyper involved in our church. It was the hive of activity where almost all of our relationships were formed. I almost never spent time alone; instead my life was full of things to do with people I considered myself connected to.

For more than a decade I allowed busyness to blind me to the true condition of my life. And then, the earth seemed to literally shift beneath my feet.

Jason took a new job in a different state. He would no longer be working for a church and would telecommute, allowing us to stay in our community. In order to make room for the person who would replace him, we left our church but assumed the relationships we had built there would remain intact. Sadly, we were wrong.

It was as if someone pulled an emergency brake on our schedules and we went from having every day, evening, and weekend full of things to do to suddenly having nothing going on. Our phones stopped ringing. The relationships that had once filled every crevice of our lives simply faded away.

Don't worry; you haven't picked up a book written by a bitter former pastor's wife. There was no nasty church stink that caused us to be cut off from our former friends. But I believe that what we experienced in that season is symptomatic of the way that many of us live our modern lives. I have a hunch that you know how it feels to have many friends, a full schedule, and a pit in your stomach. There is an illusion of connectedness to the people around you accompanied by a gnawing fear that you're somehow alone in this world.

After we left our church, loneliness hit me like a tidal wave. I felt so disoriented in my new reality that I began referring to that season as "the seismic shift." I felt suddenly and painfully aware that I had settled for the *mirage* of connectedness. I had chosen to keep my relationships at a surface level because that was easier. It simply required less of me to remain in shallow waters than it would to develop deep friendships. As a result, when the convenience factor was removed, those relationships, while amicable, simply ceased to exist.

Once the bubble burst I looked hard into the condition of my permanent relationships. My marriage, my relationships with my siblings and my parents, my most important friendships . . . I realized that while I loved those people deeply, and they loved me, I wasn't sure we really knew each other well. Something seemed to be missing.

> God has hardwired us for deep and meaningful relationships, and true connection with others is possible and game changing. #connected

By definition, a seismic shift is an event of enormous proportions with significant consequences. Watching the bottom fall out of my relationships certainly qualifies, but mine is not a sob story. While I didn't enjoy the time I spent wrestling with loneliness, I learned so much in that season, namely that God has hardwired us for deep and meaningful relationships, and true connection with others is possible and game changing.

My Own Lonely Confession

I've never won a Golden Globe, but I do know what it's like to stand on a stage and make a lonely confession. I was scheduled to speak at a large event for teen girls and their adult leaders smack-dab in the middle of the seismic shift. I can't remember what I had planned to speak on but as I was preparing my notes to teach, I felt the Lord gently nudge me to shift gears and speak on the subject of loneliness. If I had my way, I would have stuck to something less personal. Something that made me sound like I had my act together. But I've learned through the years that obedience to the nudges of God is the surest way to avoid a total train wreck, so I stood on that stage and I admitted that I was lonely. I even choked down a few tears. A friend of mine who was in the audience said she started to panic when she realized I was going to cry in front of all of those people.

"I thought, Erin *never* cries," she told me later. "I had no idea what you were doing up there."

Loneliness Lesson #2: If the people in your inner circle have never watched your heart break, your mask is glued on too tightly.

I don't really remember all that I said from that stage, but I do remember what happened afterward. As I wrapped up, I asked if anyone would be brave enough to admit that while sitting in an auditorium filled with people, they felt alone. One by one, women of all ages stood. Tears streamed down their faces. I simply watched in wonder.

For almost an hour after that event, women and teenagers stood in line to talk to me. Many of them shared about what made them lonely. Some had heartbreaking stories of loss and broken relationships, but most of them simply weren't sure how to truly connect in a world that travels at lightning speed. One woman walked up to me with huge tears in her eyes and handed me a crumpled piece of paper. Hours later as I settled into my hotel room, I pulled that slip of paper from my pocket and read her bittersweet words.

"I'm lonely too."

That's it. That's all she wrote. Maybe that was all she had the courage to say, but it was as if she had handed me the key to unlocking one of the best-kept secrets of our times.

Her words were a spark that lit a fire in my belly. Suddenly I felt like a scientist in one of those movies about a crippling and contagious disease hitting the globe. Through the microscope of my own life, I discovered a pandemic of loneliness among women who seemed to have it all together, and I became determined to do something about it.

The Pandemic of Loneliness

What is a pandemic, exactly? Since my last science class was the zoology class that effectively weeded me out of the dental hygiene program my freshman year of college, I had to consult my favorite scientist, Google, to know if I'd really unlocked a phenomenon of pandemic proportions.

Here's what Dr. Google said:

- A pandemic affects large numbers of people.
- It is not constrained by social status or geographical borders.
- It is caused by something (unpleasant) spreading like wildfire.[2]

Turns out I didn't need to pass freshman zoology after all. (Take that, Professor Smith!)

Does loneliness affect large numbers of people? You betcha! I believe that many of us are lonely, even if we never use that word to describe the condition of our relationships.

Is loneliness limited to a certain group or area? Nope. Social scientists report that teenagers are lonelier than they've ever been. So are the elderly. What about the middle aged? Yep, they're lonely too. And it doesn't seem to matter where you live or how much money you've got in the bank. Loneliness has a way of jumping over all geographical and social boundaries.

Is loneliness spreading like wildfire? A recent study found that a decade ago, 10 percent of Americans self-identified themselves as lonely. Today, that number has doubled and nearly 40 percent of Americans report a desire to find a place among a few good friends.[3]

Despite a surge in social media and gadget-assisted connectedness, loneliness is spreading. And without taking a hard look at the problem, more and more of us will soon be infected.

So, we've got a lonely pandemic on our hands. What's the big deal? Why does that matter?

The Aftershocks of Loneliness

When I talk about loneliness, I'm not referring to an empty Friday night with nothing to do and only a good chick flick to keep us company. (Sign me up for *that* kind of loneliness any day!) I'm talking about chronic loneliness. A kind of loneliness that has little to do with whether or not you have people in your world to spend time with. It's a sense that no one really knows you or understands you. One of the women we interviewed for this book summed it up this way, "Loneliness is knowing that people aren't thinking about me." It's the feeling that you must face the rough edges of life alone. That your heart is untethered to the hearts of others.

That kind of loneliness does more than simply motivate us to make a few new friends or throw a barbecue in our back yard.

The medical community is beginning to study the effect of chronic loneliness. Here's what they discovered in the bodies of lonely people.

- Vascular resistance—Researchers have found that the lonelier patients are, the greater their body's resistance to the flow of blood being pushed through their circulatory system. As a result the hearts of lonely people must work harder than the non-lonely and their blood vessels are often damaged.[4]

- Increased stress—Lonely individuals produce much higher levels of cortisol, a hormone that indicates stress.[5]
- Decreased immunity.[6]
- Faster progression of Alzheimer's disease.[7]
- Impaired ability to regulate behavior.[8]
- Greater predisposition to depression and alcoholism.[9]
- Increased risk of suicide.[10]
- Less efficient sleep—sleep becomes less restorative.[11]

Loneliness isn't simply an emotion. It works like a disease that attacks the most essential functions of our bodies.

> Loneliness isn't simply an emotion. It works like a disease that attacks the most essential functions of our bodies. #connected

In fact, researchers have discovered that among the lonely there is increased inflammatory signaling coming out of the nucleus of the cell.[12] Translation: When we're lonely the very core of our being screams out that something is wrong. Every part of us, down to the smallest particle of our cells starts sending out warning signals.

Dr. John Cacioppo is a neuroscientist leading the charge in understanding the medical impact of our chronic loneliness. He summed up his findings this way:

> Doctors have underestimated the importance of loneliness. We have characterized individuals as rugged individualists. We praised the solitary scientist or the noble athlete who spends, you know, time training and then excelling as an individual at their sport. There's nothing wrong with that, but it leads us sometimes to underestimate the importance of being connected. We are fundamentally a social species. Our capacity doesn't derive from our individual mind. Our capacity derives from our ability to work as a collective.[13]

While we may give trophies and honors to those who go at it alone, our bodies are telling a different story. We are built for connection. There are serious, life-threatening consequences when we live in a chronic state of disconnectedness. In short, our loneliness is killing us.

Patmos Syndrome

Let me preface my next statement by saying I love the church. This is not a book on everything the church is doing wrong, or how Christianity has messed things up for the masses. I believe that the church holds the only vaccine to our lonely problem. But sometimes, our Christian communities elevate a solitary faith. God is supposed to be all that we need after all, right?

I call it the Patmos Syndrome. We elevate John, isolated on the island of Patmos, as somehow more holy or more spiritual than John when he was part of a pack of disciples. We hold high those saints who go at it alone and willingly choose isolation for the sake of the kingdom.

But what if we've got it all wrong? What if God wanted us to be connected to others so much that He hardwired the craving to connect into our very DNA? What if we gave ourselves permission to need others? Would we become vaccinated against the pandemic of loneliness? Would we have the power to vaccinate others?

Suit Up

Spoiler alert: I'm not lonely anymore. I don't have to wonder if I'm known and understood. I've traded in the substitutes of busyness, technology, and surface friendships for knowing and being known. Chronic loneliness doesn't have to be a part of the human condition or the Christian faith. But that shift took hard work and required me to do some deep digging into God's Word for answers.

Like any good scientist, I left no stone unturned. In fact, my friends and I traveled all over the country talking to women just like you in our search for answers. We found lonely women in all shapes and sizes. We also found incredible stories of hope that you will read in the pages of this book.

In the mad science lab of my own life, I also conducted a few experiments. I spent a month avoiding anything automated (think ATMs and pay-at-the-pump) to see if all of the conveniences of modern life are somehow robbing us of connection. You'll love the people I met along the way. I gave up social media for a month and lived to tell the tale. Is our technology making us lonely? I think I know the answer and I'll share it with you. I also visited the truly lonely. Their stories will give you perspective and help you see what's really on the line if we remain a lonely people.

So, whadya say? Are you ready to zip up a hazmat suit of your own and join me in pushing back against the pandemic of loneliness? I should warn you, it's messy at times (as dealing with our junk always is). But we've all seen the movies where a pandemic threatens our collective way of life. Eventually, a cure is discovered and the people are saved from an ominous threat. It makes for a great blockbuster and an even better script for our lives.

God offers hope for the lonely in His Word. There is another way. Let's get busy and discover the cure together.

CHAPTER 2

The Loneliest Man to Ever Live

"Then the LORD God said, 'It is not good that the man should be alone; I will make him a helper fit for him'" (Gen. 2:18).

Adam may well be the Guinness World Record holder for loneliness. He did spend some time as the only person on the face of the Earth after all. His story has much to teach us about God's intended design for us. Ultimately, Adam's story has the power to answer the big question: Do we *need* relationships?

We can become a little too familiar with the story of Adam and Eve. Fabulous garden. Check. Lying serpent. Yep. Fig leaves, forbidden fruit, the fall . . . got it. If we spend much time in church at all, we learn the basics of Genesis 1–3 pretty well. But sometimes we can miss some nuances of the story with huge implications for our lives outside the garden walls.

Real quick, put this book down and pick up your Bible. (Don't worry; I'll wait right here.) Read Genesis 1–3 and ask the Lord to show you any lessons you may have missed about the ways mankind has always been wired for relationships.

Loneliness versus Being Alone

Although Adam was the only human being on the face of the entire planet, he was not alone. God Himself talked to Adam (Gen. 2:16). There was an intimacy present between the Creator and His creation from the very beginning. And God provided all that Adam might need. Adam had a companion and a provider in God and yet, something was off. I imagine that it felt much like the sense that many of us have about our own lives. There are people around us. Our basic needs are met, but something just isn't right.

> There are people around us. Our basic needs are met, but something just isn't right.
> #connected

In Genesis 2:19–20, God parades a menagerie of creatures before Adam. Adam is given the unique and exciting privilege of naming every animal that God had formed. He was surrounded by beasts and birds, furry creatures to snuggle and slimy things to admire from afar. But look at the lives of those crazy cat ladies on TLC and it's obvious that animals, no matter how cute or how many, are not an adequate substitute for human connection. Zoom in. Look a little closer at this part of the story. It seems that the animal parade was really an object lesson in understanding God's plan for relationships.

Before He brought a single animal to Adam, God said, "It is not good that the man should be alone; I will make him a helper fit for him" (Gen. 2:18).

As another sign of the intimacy between Adam and God, God graciously considered Adam's solitude. We have no indication that Adam complained about feeling lonely. He didn't ask God for more than He already had. But God knew that Adam needed a companion. He knew because He had made Adam to need others.

I don't think that God's plan was ever for the animals to fill this void in Adam's heart. It doesn't align with the character of God to imagine the naming of the animals as a massive exercise in trial and error.

"Maybe the lion will be a good mate. Nope. Too carnivorous. Perhaps the spider will keep Adam from being lonely. Ah. Too creepy? I guess you're right. Maybe a fish will do. But alas it needs to be in the water all the time and I didn't equip Adam with gills . . ."

Adam's naming of the animals was not a matching game gone wrong.

Verse 20 says, "The man gave names to all livestock and to the birds of the heavens and to every beast of the field. But for Adam there was not found a helper fit for him."

God knew that the animals could not fill the void in Adam's life, but Adam didn't. Adam was surrounded, and yet no matter how hard he tried, he could not find a creature that "got him." No one was enough like him.

"Though there was an upper world of angels and a lower world of brutes, and he between them, yet there being none of the same nature and rank of beings with himself not that he could converse familiarly with, he might be truly said to be alone."[1]

When God surveyed all that He had made only one thing displeased Him. Only one part of all of creation received His stamp of disapproval that it was "not good." It was Adam's loneliness.

What God says of Adam, Solomon says of all men: "Two are better than one, because they have a good reward for their toil" (Eccl. 4:9).

Solomon really was wiser than most. He recognized that being connected is far better than being disconnected. That being a part of a pair, or a family, or a circle of friends produces a "good reward" in our lives.

The Big Swap

God could have created Adam and Eve out of the same sand sculpture. Adam didn't need to spend any time alone. I believe there was a delay between the creation of the first man and the creation of his mate to teach us all a lesson: It's okay to need each other.

In 1 Corinthians 12:21 Paul is describing the members of the body of Christ (a.k.a. Christians) when he writes these words, "The eye cannot say to the hand, 'I have no need of you,' nor again the head to the feet, 'I have no need of you.'"

A spirit of independence just doesn't fly when we think of the human body. No part can go at it alone. Likewise, when we arch our backs and determine to face this life without needing others, without letting others into our homes and our hearts, without relying on others for help, we are fooling ourselves. It simply doesn't work.

We have a tendency to revert to our own version of the animal parade. We try to swap other things for human connection and connection with God, but no suitable match will ever be found. The things of this world— including our busyness, our iStuff, our achievements, our acquaintances, our appointments, and our independent streaks—cannot make a helpmeet fit for us.

Adam Says, "I Do."

"So the LORD God caused a deep sleep to fall upon the man, and while he slept took one of his ribs and closed up its place with flesh. And the rib that the LORD God had taken from the man he made into a woman and brought her to the man" (Gen. 2:21–22).

God provided Eve for Adam. Maybe God forced Adam to sleep through the creation process so that there would be no illusion that Adam drummed up the woman for himself. God created the need for connection then *He* provided the solution.

> God created the need for connection then *He* provided the solution.
> #connected

With this truth in mind, one verse jumps out at me from the Genesis account: "Therefore a man shall leave his father and his mother and hold fast to his wife, and they shall become one flesh" (Gen. 2:24).

God gives permission here to "cleave" or to hold on tightly to human relationships but He must be talking about more than Adam and Eve in this verse. You see,

Adam and Eve had no father or mother to leave. They were not born of a man and a woman; God created them. So all of that leaving father and mother to hold fast to another business must have been prescriptive, not descriptive. God was talking about us.

When it comes to our relationships, God intends for us to cling. We have a tendency to distort things. We conjure up images of being a clingy girl who is whiny and needy and we say "no thanks." But what if we are throwing the baby out with the bathwater? What if by refusing to be needy we deny God the opportunity to meet a deep, genuine need?

In Matthew Henry's commentary on Genesis 2, he writes, "Perfect solitude would turn a paradise into a desert, and a palace into a dungeon."[2]

And yet solitude is what we often choose. We isolate ourselves. We neglect our relationships with God and with others and then we wonder why we feel so sad.

God met Adam's need for relationship, and everything was rainbows and butterflies and romantic walks on the beach for a while. Ah ha! So the answer to our loneliness problem must be a great marriage, right?

Not exactly.

"In marriage I am lonely a lot of the time. I don't want to talk to my family about what's going on in my marriage because you don't want to put your spouse in a bad light. I have found myself at a crossroads where I've become an introvert because I don't have anyone to talk to." (Kailey, age 24)

"The loneliest I have ever been is when I was married. I didn't have the luxury of being married to someone who wanted to invest in me and be my best friend. They just wanted to have me there to have a wife. We put on a show. I learned to put on a happy face. I was very alone. I was not a priority and was not being invested in spiritually." (Rachel, age 25)

"My loneliest moments are when I'm with [my husband] but I'm not connected to him. When he disappears in his own hole emotionally and when he stops talking, I feel disconnected. That can go on for days and I feel like it's never going to end." (Amy, age 37)

We girls can be a bipolar bunch. Either we withdraw and isolate ourselves, keeping our relationships at the surface level to keep things neat and tidy, or we put all of our eggs in one basket, looking to others—especially the men in our lives—to fill every single relational void.

Neither path will take us somewhere pleasant.

Adam didn't trade in his relationship with God for his relationship with his wife. He had both. He needed both.

Only God can supply all of our needs (Phil. 4:19). When we neglect our relationship with Him, we will find ourselves very lonely but one way God provides is through human connection. When we refuse to accept that gift or look to our human relationships to be everything we need, we will find ourselves badly off-kilter.

The Keys to Paradise

A bit more Matthew Henry commentary . . . (What can I say, it's good stuff!)

"He that has a good God, a good heart, and a good wife, to converse with, and yet complains he wants conversation, would not have been easy and content in paradise; for Adam himself had no more . . . Those that are most satisfied in God and his favour are in the best way, and in the best frame to receive the good things of this life and shall be sure of them."[3]

Adam shows us a foundational truth about our human connection. Adam needed intimate connection with God *and* he needed intimate connection with another person. If Adam's relationship with God or with his wife was strained, Adam suffered.

Do we need relationships? Yes, we do. Admitting that can feel radical in a culture that values strong-willed independence. But first and foremost we need a relationship with Adam and Eve's God, and we must learn to trust Him to teach us what this relationship business is really all about.

CHAPTER 3

Known versus Loved

What do these three women have in common?

Whitney Houston

Marilyn Monroe

Princess Diana

Did you guess tragic deaths? That would certainly be true. Were they public figures with secrets in their private lives? Maybe. Are they among the world's most beautiful women? I'd say so, but that's not the connection that interests me most. These women were loved. Very, very loved. They had huge fan bases and their names up in lights and paparazzi waiting in the bushes to give the world more of them. Yep, these women were *loved*, but would they have traded in all the love in the world for a chance to be *known* instead? If I were a betting gal, I'd go all in on answering "yes."

Let's use Whitney as an example. Her hits like "I Wanna Dance with Somebody" and "I Will Always Love You" would be on the soundtrack for my life, for sure. Her career spanned three decades. She sold over

200 million records. She holds the Guinness World Record for the most awarded female act of all time.[1] Yes, Whitney Houston was loved. But she died alone in a hotel bathtub.

How about Marilyn? She was one of the biggest stars of all times. Loved and desired by generations and yet she, too, died alone, found dead in her bedroom by her maid.

> There is a difference between being known and being loved. All too often we hang our hopes on the wrong hook. #connected

Princess Diana was The People's Princess. She was killed when the paparazzi's desire to feed the public's craving for more of her resulted in a tragic crash. Was it the people's love that eventually killed her?

These graphic images illustrate an important reality—there is a difference between being known and being loved. All too often we hang our hopes on the wrong hook.

Daisies and T-Top Corvettes

I was just about to start cooking supper when my mom called out of the blue.

"Can we come pick up the boys and take them to the movies?"

Hot diggity! My night just got a lot more interesting!

Jason and I waved goodbye to our three boys and hopped in the car. Where were we going? We didn't know. What would we do when we got there? Who cares! We were kid-free and ready to party. Don't get me wrong, we love our kids, but life with three small boys isn't exactly conducive to romance. There are always messes to clean up, fights to referee, snacks to dish out. It seems that we go days without ever talking about more than who will handle pick-ups, drop-offs, baths, and bedtime stories. That's why, when we get a little time together, we always default to one of our favorite games. As we cruised the back roads, giddy to be in a vehicle without car seats, Jason and I settled into a familiar rhythm.

Jason: Favorite flower?

Me: Daisy.

Jason: Favorite color?

Me: Yellow.

Jason: Favorite car?

Me: T-top Corvette.

Jason: Musician you most want to see in concert?

Me: Elvis.

He already knows the answers to the questions. He's been asking them for decades. But every question is like a love note that says, "I know you." Few people have known me longer than he has. No one has known me deeper. But I need the reminder that I am known. He needs reminded of the delight found in the knowing.

Hallmark's got it all wrong. Being known is far more romantic than being loved. Unfortunately, that's a memo our culture seems to have missed. We're obsessed with being loved. We think admiration, adulation, and applause is the be-all and end-all. I'm not saying that love doesn't matter or that we don't need it, of course we do. But love is cheap. *Knowing* is the good stuff we should all be after.

Souls Knit Together

David was a superstar in his day. He was certainly loved. Throngs of women cheered his name in the street (1 Sam. 18:7). But what did that love gain him? Let's take a quick look at David, and the people who loved him.

King Saul

In 1 Samuel 17, David impresses Saul by offering to whip up on the oppressive enemy soldier Goliath. I'm sure you've heard the story. David hits the giant with a rock, cuts off his head, and brings it to the king.

Apparently, dismembered body parts was Saul's love language, because he is immediately enamored with David. He does not allow David to return home, but brings him to the palace.

But Saul's love was short lived.

Saul became insanely jealous of David. He plotted to kill him several times. Eventually Saul's rage burned so hot that David was forced to flee.

Cue Poison's "Every Rose Has Its Thorn" . . .

Michal

Michal loved David too.

"Now Saul's daughter Michal loved David. And they told Saul, and the thing pleased him" (1 Sam. 18:20).

Michal loved David so much that she wanted to marry him, and so she did. But as we all know, marital love doesn't always result in happily ever after. If we fast-forward in David's story a bit we read, "As the ark of the LORD came into the city of David, Michal the daughter of Saul looked out of the window and saw King David leaping and dancing before the LORD, *and she despised him in her heart*" (2 Sam. 6:16, emphasis mine).

Cue Carly Simon's "You're So Vain" . . .

Saul and Michal loved David. At times they really, really loved David, but the love didn't last. Eventually, it was replaced with jealousy and resentment. If the long list of songs written about love gone wrong is any indication, most of us have experienced this kind of love on the rocks.

Jonathan

Jonathan was Saul's son and David's best friend. The Bible tells us that Jonathan gave David his robe, armor, sword, bow, and belt. These were friendship offerings given from one warrior to another. When Saul intended to kill David, Jonathan worked as a mediator. When his dad could not be dissuaded, Jonathan helped David escape.

David and Jonathan's friendship provides the definition we need to understand being known.

1 Samuel 18:1 tells us, "As soon as he had finished speaking to Saul, *the soul of Jonathan was knit to the soul of David*, and Jonathan loved him as his own soul" (emphasis mine).

Knit-together souls. This is the image of knowing.

Knowing says, "I see who you are and choose to weave my life into yours." How much better does that sound than simply, "I love you"?

Knitting Lessons

I am constantly in search of the perfect hobby. I've tried violin, drums, embroidery, and decoupage. My knitting phase was particularly ill-fated.

I have a friend who is a master knitter. She makes our whole family wool socks each year for Christmas. Putting them on is like wearing a hug for my feet. I asked her to teach me her craft. Bless her heart. She tried. She really did.

I hated it! I got far more stitches wrong then I got right. My pot holder looked like something a squirrel had spent the winter in. It didn't take long for me to throw down my knitting needles and decide there was far too much counting and concentration involved. I paid my dues in Math for Dummies in college; I certainly was not going to pick it up again as a hobby.

I didn't become a knitter, but I am thankful for my knitting lessons. When I read that Jonathan's soul was knit to David's, I understand the analogy. This was a relationship that took intentionality. It required concentrated effort. That's why knit-together souls are such a beautiful description of knowing. It is the process of mining someone else's heart to discover all the jewels within. It is seeing someone for who they really are and willfully super gluing your own self to them.

Sometimes, we are lonely because we are so wrapped up in loving and being loved that we miss the opportunity to know and be known.

Sometimes, we are lonely because we are so wrapped up in loving and being loved that we miss the opportunity to know and be known.

> Knowing and being known only happens when we allow the roots of our relationships to grow deep. #connected

No. That wasn't a typo. I wrote that sentence twice because I want it to permeate your heart. I want you to realize that being loved is not the same as being known. Just ask David, Whitney, Marilyn, and Diana. Love is based on what you can do for each other and what you look like when your best foot is pointing forward. Knowing and being known only happens when we allow the roots of our relationships to grow deep.

A Knowing God

God is in the business of making Himself known. It's a truth written all over the Bible. Here are the highlights.

- The Lord has made Himself known. (Ps. 9:16)
- God makes the path of life known. (Ps. 16:11)

- He makes His covenant known. (Ps. 25:14)
- We can know Him as our fortress. (Ps. 48:3)
- God's ways can be known on earth. (Ps. 67:2)
- The wonders of God can be known. (Ps. 88:12)
- God makes His faithfulness known. (Ps. 89:1)
- God makes His salvation known. (Ps. 98:2)
- He is known as a mighty power. (Ps. 106:8)
- He reveals "hidden things" we cannot know without Him. (Isa. 48:6; Jer. 33:3)
- Jesus came to make God known. (John 1:18)

If you're like me, you tend to race through bulleted lists like that, but I encourage you to go back and read that list slowly. Let your mind land on this radical truth—the God of the universe lets me know *Him*.

After you've picked up all the pieces of your brain from that mind-blowing truth, consider this—the God of the universe knows *you*.

Here's proof:

- God knows the distress of your soul. (Ps. 31:7)
- Before you ever speak a word, God knows what you will say. (Ps. 139:4)
- He knows the exact number of days you will live. (Ps. 139:16)
- If anyone loves God, he is known by God. (1 Cor. 8:3)

- He knows the number of hairs on your head. (Luke 12:7)

Galatians 4:9 says, "But now . . . you have come to know God, or rather to be known by God."

Psalm 139:1 says, "O LORD, you have searched me and known me!"

In many ways, Christianity is a lifelong study of God, but when it comes to us, He's already done His homework. He knows you intimately. He knit you together and then studied His handiwork. He invites you to weave your story into His.

When Jason works to know me better, I recognize it as a sweet gift. How lucky am I to have found a man willing to mine my heart for decades? (He's mine. You cannot have him.) If you find yourself chronically lonely, you might be missing something huge! That same sweetness can be found from God. He knows you. He invites you to know Him in return.

A Hint of What's to Come

If you've been to many Christian weddings, you know the love chapter of the Bible. First Corinthians 13 tells us what love should look like, but the chapter is wrapped in a strange bow: "For now we see in a mirror dimly, but then face to face. Now I know in part; then I shall know fully, even as I have been fully known" (1 Cor. 13:12).

After a vivid description of what love is, Paul seems to take a hard left turn here into the subject of being known. For now, our concept of love is a little hazy, our concept of knowing perhaps even hazier. Knowing God has to be squeezed through the filter of sin and sometimes things get lost in translation. But . . .

A day is coming when we will know Him fully. Love is like the appetizer to the best feast we will ever enjoy.

God's love is a precious gift, but the reason He loves me is even more beautiful. He loves me because He knows me. He knows every hair on my head, every thought in my brain, every worry in my heart. He sees all of me, from beginning to end, and He loves me. He invites me to knit my heart into His in a bond so tight that we can never be pulled apart. Being so intimately known is the vaccination we all need to cure our deep feelings of loneliness.

Don't Settle

I hope you're starting to realize that dealing with the pandemic of loneliness isn't going to be easy. We can't simply make a new friend or cram more people into church pews and see the tide start to turn. Our relationships with God and others are as intertwined as a big ol' plate of spaghetti. We've got to reexamine some of our most basic understandings of who He is and how He made us in order to connect. I'm afraid we've been singing a song all wrong since preschool. Yes, Jesus loves me, this I know. But when loneliness comes, I need to be reminded that Jesus *knows* me. This I love.

> Yes, Jesus loves me, this I know. But when loneliness comes, I need to be reminded that Jesus *knows* me. This I love. #connected

Yes, God loves you and that is a beautiful truth, but maybe we find ourselves unsatisfied because we've missed the wonder of His knowing. Is it possible that has trickled down into our other relationships—causing us to crave love while missing opportunities to knit our souls with others?

Many of us have experienced deep heartache, starting in childhood. If we started to compare relationship scars, I'd have some big ones to show. I get that being known can be very, very scary. Relationships are complicated. Knowing and being known doesn't always work out like a Lifetime Original movie. Sometimes we step on land mines, and the whole thing gets blown to bits.

But loneliness doesn't effectively insulate us from pain, does it? It just transfers the hurt to another corner of our hearts.

When it comes to dealing with loneliness, we are just getting warmed up. God's Word is a deep well with the answers to our ache to connect. We'll get there. But for now, I'd like you to consider this:

- Do I seek to know God? Am I comfortable with Him knowing me?
- Do I crave love and admiration instead of knowing and being known?
- Do I knit my life to others? Do I allow them to knit their lives into mine?

CHAPTER 4

Entering the
Blanket Fort

On a particularly cold and nasty winter day, my kids and I decided to banish cabin fever by building a blanket fort. Actually the fort was all their idea, but they recruited me to help set up the card table and drag out every pillow and blanket we own. When we were finished, my boys retreated to their newly created dark cave and I plopped onto the couch. They kept popping their heads out between the quilts to invite me to come inside, but I was hesitant. Instead, I checked my iPhone for any news. News of what, I'm not sure. I had no reason to expect a big announcement, but that didn't keep me from incessantly checking Twitter and e-mail. I guess I was hoping the virtual people in my life would offer me something my flesh-and-blood, sitting-in-the-same-room-as-me family could not.

It occurred to me in that moment that technology has blunted my appetite for human connection. The pixels had become more alluring than the real thing. The illusion seemed more inviting than reality. I felt like an addict whose drug of choice was a little box of glass and metal. The high came through full in-boxes, favorites, and re-Tweets, and I needed more and more to get the same rush.

The truth is that the illusion of human connection online just leaves me addicted, never satisfied. I wish I had entered the blanket fort instead.

No Witch Hunts Here

If we are going to talk about the ways loneliness rears its ugly head in our modern lives, we must take a hard look at technology. Don't worry. There will be no witch hunt for your iStuff. I won't propose a ceremonial burning of everything with an on/off switch or suggest that if we all moved to a TV-free hippie commune, then loneliness would cease to exist in our lives.

The reality is that technology is both a cause of loneliness and a false cure. It's impacting our relationships and the impact overall isn't good. But technology is here to stay. Over-romanticizing life without a screen won't scratch our itch to be known. The answer is to rethink the difference between authentic human connection and connection to the virtual world. For the briefest of moments let's walk away from our technology (unless you are reading this on your e-reader, then by all means, keep reading!) and see what we can learn by stepping into the blanket fort.

> The reality is that technology is both a cause of our loneliness and a false cure. #connected

The Big Breakup

When faced with the fact that I am a technology addict, I decided to quit cold turkey by breaking up with my screens for one month. I sat my gadgets down and gave them the "It's not you, it's me" talk. Because really, the fact that I'm addicted is my problem. The technology itself is not the issue.

The parameters of our breakup were simple. No TV. No Twitter. No unnecessary surfing online (Facebook and I had broken up years ago). For one month I would seek to spend my time with actual people without the barrier of a screen.

You should know that I'm a bit of a technology hermit anyway. Actually, that TV-free hippie commune I mentioned earlier is my dream. For our entire marriage, my husband and I have had a tug-of-war over TV. I want to live TV-free. I like to imagine myself baking bread and canning vegetables instead of vegging out on the couch in front of the tube. My man doesn't share my fantasy, and so for more than a decade we have moved a TV in and out of our lives. The reality is that I watch plenty of television on my laptop and would usually prefer to spend my free time being entertained than pretending I'm Ma from *Little House on the Prairie*. Even so, pulling the plug on television watching was pretty easy for me.

Turning the TV off permanently might prove more painful for others. Three-fourths of people over fifty say their main source of company in the evenings is the TV. Half of young people say the same thing.[1] *The Bachelor* has become our bestie. Those real housewives feel like our real friends. If television is your technology drug of choice, you may have withdrawals at the idea of my month without it. I get it. I do and so does the rest of the world. TV can feel like a legitimate solution to our craving to be known. But somehow we all sense that we're settling when we look to sitcoms and reality TV to meet our relational needs, don't we?

TV may not have a hold on me, but his nasty little cousin, the smartphone, certainly does.

"My name is Erin and I'm an iPhone addict."

I felt like I needed an AA-like intervention as I tried to go one month without my iPhone. We might need something like group therapy to pry our eyes from our digital media. Researchers have found that we consume an average of 5 hours and 9 minutes of digital media per day, eclipsing our average TV viewing time (4 hours and 31 minutes per day). They also say our total media time is somewhere around 12 hours per day.[2] No wonder I'm so tired and my house is so messy. Who has time to sleep or vacuum with so much screen time?

Day 1 of my technology fast, I must have checked Twitter at least ten times. What was wrong with me? What's so great about a bunch of people I've never met sending me links to articles I will never read?

You may read that sentence and think, "Twitter is so last year." When it comes to new technology, we all have whiplash. Things are moving at warp speed, but the essence has always been the same—connect us with other people (real or imagined) in a way that is fast, convenient, and taps into our fantasy version of ourselves. There's a biological reason all that social networking is so fun. It's the same reason I couldn't bear to break up with my iStuff even for a single month. I'll tell you what happens in your brain every time you swipe that little button on your home screen in a minute.

I bought my phone a little "hotel" (i.e., tiny Rubbermaid) where he could spend the month. In case of a Twitter emergency, I would be forced to break the glass, or at least pry the lid off. I thought if I had to actually open a box to get to my phone, I would remember my experiment and my mission to cure the pandemic of loneliness and I would resist. But I'm an addict, remember? To addicts, going without their drug of choice feels like an emergency, so I pried that little plastic box open plenty to get a hit.

This wasn't working. I had to get serious. I went to Walmart and bought a dumb phone. No wireless. No e-mail. Not even any fancy ringtones. Just a phone. I survived two whole days with that little beauty before I returned it, raced back home, busted my iPhone out of its "hotel" and returned to my virtual relationships.

There May Not Be a Pot of Gold

Pulling the plug on technology isn't easy. And you know what else? It doesn't automatically mean our loneliness will disappear.

You would think that with the free time secured by being online less, I would nurture my human relationships more. I would take more walks, do crafts with my kids, discuss the meaning of life over coffee with my husband. But that's not what happened. I may be putting too much relational stock in the virtual world, but I am isolated for much bigger reasons than the invention of the smartphone. We all are.

Paul Miller would agree. Paul is a technology journalist (as in an uber technology junkie) who decided to go one year Internet free. Paul figured when the withdrawals passed, pulling the plug would help him discover the deep connectedness he'd been missing. But that's not what happened. This is what he wrote at the end of his one-year Internet fast:

> One year ago I left the Internet. I thought it was making me unproductive. I thought it lacked meaning. I thought it was "corrupting my soul."
>
> It's been a year now since I "surfed the web" or "checked my email" or "liked" anything with a figurative rather than literal thumbs-up. I've managed to stay disconnected, just like I planned. I'm Internet free.
>
> And now I'm supposed to tell you how it solved all my problems. I'm supposed to be enlightened. I'm supposed to be more "real," now. More perfect.
>
> But instead it's 8 p.m. and I just woke up. I slept all day, woke with eight voicemails on my phone from friends and coworkers. I went to my coffee shop to consume dinner, the Knicks game, my two newspapers, and a copy of *The New Yorker*. And now I'm watching *Toy Story* while I glance occasionally at the blinking cursor in this text document, willing it to write itself, willing it to generate the epiphanies my life has failed to produce.

I didn't want to meet this Paul at the tail end of my yearlong journey.[3]

Paul didn't find a pot of gold filled with deep, meaningful relationships at the end of the technology-free rainbow, and neither did I. After a month of trying to use my technology less, I gained thirty Twitter followers (proving that I truly am more interesting when I keep my mouth shut) and simply found other ways to check out and disengage.

I admit that technology is not the only reason we're feeling so disconnected. Even so, it is taking a toll. It's true that technology is changing us and our relationships and we need to examine how, but the answer is to be smart consumers of our screens and wise investors in our relationships, not to decide that technology is the only reason we're all feeling so alone together.

Just the Facts, Ma'am

When I tell people I'm not on Facebook and don't own a TV, they always get a little . . . squirmy. They almost always default to one of these defenses:

"Well, I almost never watch TV."

"I'm only on Facebook to keep up with people who live far away."

"I haven't been on Facebook in months."

Honestly, when I'm not writing a chapter about technology, I largely consider the media consumption habits of others to be none of my business, but I have marveled at the consistency with which others feel the need to defend themselves in this area. The fact that we're all so testy about our media usage should throw up a red flag or two. The truth is we're all addicted, and our denial about this fact isn't doing us much good.

Here are the hard facts:

- Seventy percent of Americans sleep with their cell phones within arm's length. One-third of us get online before getting out of bed.[4]
- Sixty-one percent of us check our phones every hour.[5]
- Adults spend at least eight to twelve hours per day staring at screens. That's more time than we spend on any other activity, including sleeping.[6]
- Despite the fact that most young people have an average of 243 Facebook friends, it's not translating into real-life friendships. Researchers theorize that we are spending so much time online, that we no longer have time to go out with our non-Facebook friends.[7]
- It seems that no matter which side of the pond we're on, technology has us seriously hooked. In South Korea the government has started

providing counseling programs and psychological treatment for an estimated two million people who cannot wean themselves from online computer games. Officials there are so concerned about this issue that they have mandated that children as young as three be schooled in controlling their device and Internet use.[8]

What is the result of being constantly plugged in?

More than half of us admit that we find it difficult to make friends in "real life" compared with online.[9]

"Skin hunger" is a real condition that is impacting more and more of us. Think of skin hunger as the adult version of failure to thrive.[10] It has become such an issue that MIT students invented the Like-A-Hug inflatable jacket, a garment that inflates to "hug" you whenever someone likes your Facebook post. For real. I can't make this stuff up. In 2006 the Hug Shirt was released. TIME magazine named it one of the best inventions of the year.[11] I can only assume that our skin hunger has gotten progressively worse since then. In the absence of regular, meaningful human contact we fail to reach our full potential. One study discovered that skin hunger was making young people as lonely as the elderly, the group typically seen as the loneliest among us.[12]

"Eighteen-year-olds are as lonely as eighty-year-olds and they want a friendship service because they can no longer make friends in the traditional ways," said an editor that spearheaded a study into the issue in Britain.

"Without realizing it, our society no longer provides on the basic functions that keeps it working. The everyday contact, courtesies, and kindnesses, which turn into friendship and knit us together, have been allowed to disappear in favor of efficiency. Modern society doesn't encourage us to speak to each other face to face and as a result, loneliness levels are soaring to crisis point and set to get even worse."[13]

We can downplay our usage all day long, but our gadgets tell a different story. We're addicted and our addiction is driving a wedge between us and those we are designed to connect with. When it comes to loneliness, we

> In the absence of regular, meaningful human contact we fail to reach our full potential. #connected

may well be shooting ourselves in the foot and it's possible that technology is the smoking gun.

Why We Keep Clicking

My hunch is that you already know this is true. Like me, I doubt that your technology is pulling its weight in the relationship. You know it's a cheap substitute and you probably sense that our media usage has gotten out of control. So, why do we keep clicking? I blame my brain.

Scientists have discovered that every time we get a technological "ping" such as a text or e-mail alert, our brain gets a hit of dopamine.[14]

Here's a crash course in that science. Dopamine is a neurotransmitter that runs the brain's reward and pleasure centers. It also regulates our emotional responses and helps us take action toward rewards.[15] When someone shoots us an e-mail, or sends us a friend request, or makes something we did or wrote go viral, our brains get all tingly. That feels like a reward and our brains want more of it.

What is the reward exactly? For the briefest of moments we feel known. And because our technology is so readily available and because connecting in this way is faster and more convenient than nurturing relationships in the flesh, we settle for the smaller doses of dopamine that our technology provides instead of working for the major dopamine downloads that can come from being truly connected. Our media taps into our craving to be known and applauded.

Brain researchers say that when we get low levels of dopamine, we are prone to addiction. Yes, our technology makes us feel good, but chemically speaking those warm fuzzies are seeping in at such a low level that we're all left wanting more.

There are other things happening in our brains as we click away. When we stare at a screen our heart rate slows. Our brain vessels dilate. Blood flows away from our major muscles. In other words, our body starts to relax. But the constant flow of visual stimuli can shift our orienting responses into overdrive, eventually leading to fatigue and a sense of depletion.[16]

What's more, we are feeling more and more insecure. As a result of too much time on Pinterest, women are wrestling with Mason jar envy. One *Today Show* survey revealed that seven thousand mothers worry they are not crafty or creative enough. Some admitted that they stay up all night looking at Pinterest because they're unable to stop the negative comparison. Some women admitted to developing body image issues after comparing themselves to others online. Never mind that we all know that no one really looks like their profile pic. Somehow, the constant parade of other's achievements and happy moments is messing us all up.

The results are in, folks, and the hard truth is that all that screen time is costing us.

Opportunity Cost

Think back to freshman econ and try to remember the meaning of the little term "opportunity cost." Don't worry, if you slept through economics like I did, here's a refresher course.

In microeconomic theory (yawn!) the opportunity cost of a choice is the value of the best alternative forgone.[17] In other words, when faced with two alternatives, it is the cost of what we may miss out on by choosing one over another. Everything has an opportunity cost. Wrestling with this little truth is the best way to tame our technology. Technology itself is neutral. Your iPhone isn't out to get you. Your TV isn't evil. It's possible to consume these things and not become isolated and lonely. But we've got to get real about how much technology we're really using and seriously measure the opportunity cost. What aren't we doing by spending time on Facebook, Words with Friends, Internet news, Twitter, e-mail, and watching television? Do we want to settle for the low doses of dopamine that trickle in every time we are tagged in a photo, or do we want to do the hard work to get the big download of feel-good chemicals that comes from true connection?

Society as a whole has chosen its side of the fence. The masses will continue to worship technology and work toward faster and faster (and more shallow) pings.

If you want to be truly connected, you will have to break away from the pack.

My one month free(ish) from technology did translate into a more balanced relationship with media. When I finally lifted the lid off the iPhone hotel for good, I did not automatically default to my old habits. It is possible to use technology as a means to enhance our best relationships. We don't have to be addicted. We can live modern lives with real relationships. But it requires us to put the iPhone down and enter the blanket fort, or restaurant, or church, or family where real people live and real life is happening.

Speaking of real people and real lives, it's time to turn the tables. We've talked about my technology addiction plenty. Enough about me, let's talk about you. Are you skin hungry? Are you settling for addiction to a cheap high instead of the good stuff? Here are some tough questions to answer if you're really ready to vaccinate yourself against the pandemic of loneliness.

1. How much time am I really spending looking at a screen? (Don't guess, because you will underestimate. Keep track of your actual media consumption for a few days.)

2. What pay off am I getting from technology? How can I get this same payoff from my relationships?

3. For me, what is the specific opportunity cost of my media usage?
4. Where are the "blanket forts" in my life where I can experience greater connection with others if I will make the effort?

CHAPTER 5

Lion Hunting

A herd of antelopes grazes together on an African plain. There are so many of them that they are calm and relaxed, drawing a false sense of security from their numbers. They do not scan the horizon for predators. No one stands guard. They simply eat in peace.

But look closer. Something is lurking in the tall grass.

A pride of lions is moving forward. Slowly. Meticulously. In military-like formation. They make a wide circle. Soon, they will have the herd of antelopes completely surrounded.

Suddenly one female lion gives the signal the others have been waiting for. The pride stands up in unison and starts running. The antelopes dart. A planned confusion results, and the lions work together to isolate a single doe. Then they move in for the kill and drag their prey off to the shade to be shared by the pride.[1]

It's a scene that most of us will only ever observe on Animal Planet or the National Geographic Channel. But you might be surprised how much a pride of lions hunting their prey can teach us about one of the root causes of loneliness.

Every time a lion pride hunts together it is a highly organized operation. They do not test their potential prey for weakness like other predators do. The only weakness they are looking for is isolation. If they can remove a single animal from its herd, lunch is easily delivered, even if the animal they are hunting is much larger or faster than the lions themselves.

Knowing Our Place

Where do you see yourself in the lion-hunting scene I just described? Are you the lion? Confidently stalking your prey? Are you standing on the sidelines somewhere with a telephoto lens?

The truth is, you're the antelope. So am I. Because we are all made weak and vulnerable by isolation. We may be living life, oblivious to the threat, just like the antelopes who thoughtlessly munch on grass while a lion lurks just feet away. But the threat is there and it is real. Staying disconnected has the power to do much more than make you sad or depressed. It may be just

> We are all made weak and vulnerable by isolation.
> #connected

what the Enemy uses to prey upon you and bring you down.

Back to the Garden

Let's head back to the Garden of Eden to take a look at exactly how isolation led to the fall of all mankind.

Genesis 3:1 describes Satan this way, "Now the serpent was more crafty than any other beast of the field that the LORD God had made."

While lions have earned their reputation as the king of the jungle for their cunning skills at hunting down all other animals, they may have been studying highlight reels from the serpent. The Bible describes Satan as crafty, and I don't think it's a reference to scrapbooks and hot glue guns. Satan is cunning. He will trick us. He stalks us, much like a lion pride stalks their prey.

It's no surprise then, that in 1 Peter 5:8 Peter gives us this warning: "Be sober-minded; be watchful. Your adversary the devil prowls around like a roaring lion, seeking someone to devour."

It doesn't do us any favors to envision Satan as a guy with horns and a cheap, red cape. While it may be comforting to imagine that we could see him coming and get out of his way, that's not what the Bible describes.

The facts are that as children of God, we have an Enemy. He is sneaky. He is calculating. He is looking for someone to devour. And much like the lion who leads her pride in isolating a single, unsuspecting antelope, Satan has a history of using isolation to lure us into sin and to keep us there, trapped by shame and the sense that we could never tell another soul.

In Genesis 3:1–5 the serpent, who had likely been lurking in the grass for a while, sees his opportunity and moves in for the kill.

> He said to the woman, "Did God actually say, 'You shall not eat of any tree in the garden'?" And the woman said to the serpent, "We may eat of the fruit of the trees in the garden, but God said, 'You shall not eat of the fruit of the tree that is in the midst of the garden, neither shall you touch it, lest you die.'" But the serpent said to the woman, "You will not surely die. For God knows that when you eat of it your eyes will be opened, and you will be like God, knowing good and evil."

I believe that Satan was hunting Eve. He waited for a moment when she was not surrounded by her community. Verse 6 tells us that Adam was nearby, but maybe he was just slightly out of earshot. And even if he wasn't,

Eve apparently didn't take the time to talk to him about what was happening. We see in her the very first woman with an independent streak, as she determined that she would process the information Satan was giving her and make the decision all on her own.

Would things have turned out differently for Eve if she had simply said, "Let me talk to my husband about it" before taking a bite of that rotten fruit? Certainly, she would have been double protected against this attack if she had talked to her husband *and* consulted with God. God had given her a double-layered safety net through a relationship with Him and a relationship with Adam, but she cut through the net and put herself in grave danger by deciding to go at it alone. What happened next reminds us that we are all daughters of Eve.

> Then the eyes of both were opened, and they knew that they were naked. And they sewed fig leaves together and made themselves loincloths. And they heard the sound of the LORD God walking in the garden in the cool of the day, and the man and his wife hid themselves from the presence of the LORD God among the trees of the garden. (Gen. 3:7–8)

Loneliness set Eve up to sin. Then her shame led to even deeper isolation.

Here's the big takeaway: When we step outside of community, we become infinitely more susceptible to temptation and sin. In this way, loneliness is less of an emotion, and more of a military strategy, effectively used by our Enemy. Then, our shame lies to us and tells us that isolation is the only way to regain control. In this way, loneliness and shame become a two-edged sword that is very effective at taking us out at the knees.

> When we step outside of community, we become infinitely more susceptible to temptation and sin. #connected

We heard it over and over as we interviewed women for this book. When talking about their sin they said things like:

"No one will understand."

"I will be judged."

"No one will like me."

"If people knew what I have done, they wouldn't want to be with me."

Just like Eve, these are women made vulnerable by isolation and made isolated by shame.

Antelope Stories

We talked to lots of women who told us that sin led to prolonged seasons of loneliness.

Dawn is in her early fifties. She is a single mother to a little girl she adopted. Several years ago, she was hiding a same-sex relationship. Just like Eve, her instinct was to hide, and to throw up a false front whenever she was around her Christian community. The end result was a dark and lonely valley.

"I have to say the loneliest time in my life was when I was fully immersed in sin," Dawn said. "I was surrounded by great friends who were all Christ followers, yet the guilt and shame of my wrongdoing kept me silent and secluded from seeking out any support or embrace from those who could have helped me.

"In the wake of what I had done, I felt an enormous amount of guilt and shame. I felt that I could not tell anyone because so much was at stake . . . my job, my reputation, my character, my life. I ended up resigning, choosing to 'move on' with my life in hopes that this experience would just all dissolve and go away. However, the immense weight of my sin proved to be overwhelming. I wanted desperately to tell someone, but the Enemy convinced me I needed to remain silent, convincing me that no one would understand, embrace me, or help. So, I kept quiet. And in doing that, I became so very lonely.

I went to church, but sat on the back row, spoke with no one, and never attended church events. I gathered with friends, but kept the conversation as casual as possible. And if I sensed that someone was asking questions that were getting too personal, I quickly turned the attention to someone else."

Dawn stayed on the back pew, wrapped in loneliness for eight years. Eight years of isolation. Eight years of keeping people at arm's length. Eight years of listening to the Enemy whisper that being alone was the only way to deal with her sin.

Eventually, she joined a Celebrate Recovery group where she adopted a "no more secrets" mantra, which she says led to no more shame, which led to no more loneliness.

"It took almost an entire year to get through the program," Dawn told me. "But I walked away with freedom, joy, and a firm decision that I would not be silent any longer and I would never be lonely like that again."

Eventually, Dawn got so tired of the chase that she looked the Lion in the eye and refused to be hunted. Sin had put her in a prison of isolation and telling others gave her the key to get out, but it's not always easy to place that key in the lock and turn.

There's a Hole in My Sidewalk

The bulk of my writing and speaking ministry is directed toward teenagers. As a result I often have young women contact me, looking for a lifeline when they are drowning in sin. In recent years, I've seen a huge surge in young women wrestling with pornography and masturbation. Their story is almost always the same.

Being alone sets the original trap. They have a computer or smartphone in their bedroom. The fact that no one is watching and no one would ever know makes them vulnerable to experimentation. So they Google porn. Maybe initially it's just to see what all of the fuss is about. It often only takes one hit to become addicted. Once sin has its hooks in them, shame always follows and shame always tells them to keep their secret tightly under wraps.

At some point they get desperate to escape the sin prison, and that's when I get their e-mail. I'm safe. They can't see me and I can't tell their parents. I believe that when they tell me about their sin, they're really fishing . . . sending out some bait to see how people will react to the reality that they've been eating rotten fruit. I always encourage them to tell someone else, a flesh-and-blood person in their world (as opposed to an e-mail address on the screen). They almost always resist.

Here are their actual words . . .

"I've been struggling with masturbation for twelve years of my life. I cannot tell my mum. How will I even start it? It will just break her heart. I don't know how to do it."

"I am struggling with sexual sin. It has become bigger, and bigger, and bigger. Currently, I am trying to get rid of it. It's not working. Please pray for me."

"I have recently been struggling with masturbation. But I believe I have found the strength in Christ to say 'no' to that sin. Must I tell my parents? It might break their heart. I don't feel led by God to tell them. Please help."

Until these girls tell someone, there is only one likely outcome for them. They will keep sinning. Clearly, they do not want to be addicted. They hate what they've done, and they want to be free from the shame. But they're still sewing fig leaves. Until they come out in the open and get honest about their sin with God and with their community, they will remain trapped.

My pastor recently described the progression of sin in each of our lives by reading the famous poem, "There's a Hole in My Sidewalk." Here's how it goes.

Chapter One

I walk down the street.
There's a deep hole in the sidewalk.
I fall in.

I am lost . . . I am helpless.
It isn't my fault.
It takes forever to find a way out.

Chapter Two

I walk down the same street.
There is a deep hole in the sidewalk.
I pretend I don't see it.
I fall in again.
I can't believe I am in the same place.
But it isn't my fault.
It still takes a long time to get out.

Chapter Three

I walk down the same street.
There is a deep hole in the sidewalk.
I see it is there.
I still fall in . . . it's a habit.
My eyes are open.
I know where I am.
It is my fault . . . I get out immediately.

Chapter Four

I walk down the same street.
There is a deep hole in the sidewalk.
I walk around it.

Chapter Five

I walk down another street.[2]

As the communion cups were passed in that service I thought about the holes I have fallen in over and over—those patterns of sin that most plague me. As I thought about sitting in the bottom of the sin pit, I realized that my first response is usually to look around and wonder why it's so lonely down there. Why isn't anyone coming to rescue me here? Why isn't anyone jumping into the pit with me? When sin puts us in a pit we wonder where everyone went. Maybe it's because no one knows we're down there. Instead, when we are in what the Bible describes as the "pit of destruction" (Isa. 38:17), we need to yell for help. We must make a habit of calling on others to pull us out.

> When sin puts us in a pit we wonder where everyone went. Maybe it's because no one knows we're down there. #connected

Julie has been in the sin pit. True, she isn't hiding a same-sex relationship or porn addiction. In fact, most of us would gloss over what she struggles with as a "minor sin," if we considered it a sin at all. But we would be wrong. The proof is in the fact that Julie found herself isolated, which led to sin, which kept her trapped for many years.

Julie had a major falling out with her best friend. At the same time she and her family moved to a new state for her husband's job. That job kept him away from her most of the time. In her isolated state, Julie became vulnerable and she started sipping on a cocktail of bitterness, unforgiveness, and self-pity, which eventually led to the blame game.

It was her husband's fault she felt so alone. He was gone all the time, after all. It was her former friend's fault that Julie was so lonely. Couldn't she see that Julie was the victim here?

Julie started building walls. She told herself that no one would understand her and that no one would take her side. She dwelled on unmet expectations until her heart became completely diseased by anger and resentment.

Just like Dawn, Julie eventually enrolled in a Celebrate Recovery program. There she was forced to get real about her anger and unforgiveness. And there, in the cocoon of community and as a result of confessing her sin, Julie started to feel less lonely but only after she took the hard step of *asking* others for a lifeline.

The Path of Sin

James 1:14–15 outlines the progression that sin always takes: "But each person is tempted when he is lured and enticed by his own desire. Then desire when it has conceived gives birth to sin, and sin when it is fully grown brings forth death."

This is not a happy birth story. Sin is conceived in our bellies as a result of an unholy desire. When that desire is fully developed, it is born as sin. And that sin always grows up to be a rebellious teenager that will be our undoing.

Sin starts when we are lured and enticed toward it. Satan has a history of doing the luring and enticing in moments when we are alone or feel separated from the people God has put in our lives as a safety net. But the temptation itself is not a sin. Eve could have had that conversation with the serpent with a very different outcome. The ticket to being lured and not devoured is to tell God and to tell others.

James goes on to give Christians these instructions: "Therefore, confess your sins to one another and pray for one another, that you may be healed. The prayer of a righteous person has great power as it is working" (5:16).

There is healing when we tell. There is power when we tell. There is pain and isolation when we stay silent.

A Church at the Stadium

Researchers recently surveyed those who regularly attend church services to get a feel for their experiences.

Sixty-six percent of the people they talked to said that they feel they have a "real and personal connection" with God while attending church.[3] That's good! Safety net number one is in place for many of us.

However, the study also revealed that our second layer of defense is tattered. More than a quarter of those surveyed agreed with the statement that church feels "like a group of people sharing the same space in a public event but who are not connected in a real way."[4] Another 9 percent of those surveyed weren't sure if they were connecting to others in their church or not.[5] I have to wonder if the people in this group know what connectedness feels like or if they've settled for a synthetic substitute.

What people were saying is that for them church feels like going to a football game. The stadium is packed. They are surrounded by people who all want the same thing. The mood is light, but they're not really connected. At the end of the day, the sermon, the service, the game, they will go back home to their lonely lives with the same sense that they could never tell what's really going on.

Lean in. Listen closely.

I think that this trend is less of a reflection on the state of our churches, and more evidence of a personal problem. As individuals we refuse to get real about our sin. We want to keep up appearances. We want people to think we're really good people. We prefer to think of church as a country club where we wear our best clothes, including a pretty mask, instead of a hospital where we can get bound up and healed through the loving care of others.

That kind of thinking will get us isolated from the herd every time. Sure, antelopes are pretty. People like to look at them, but they are easy targets because they are quickly separated from their community. Refusing to tell your sin to others will keep you an antelope forever.

Are you lonely? If so, is it possible that sin is the root cause? Can you look back and see that Satan waited for moments when you were outside your community? He attacked and then he lied to you and told you your shame should banish you to the bushes, making you feel even more alone.

It's time to fall into your safety net. Seek God and ask Him to reveal the sin in your life. Confess it to Him right then and there. Don't hide yourself or your junk. But don't stop there.

Tell your Christian friends. Tell your pastor. Tell your mentor. Tell your family. Keep telling until you see the lion pride slink away and set their sights on a different antelope.

CHAPTER 6

Is It Worth the Work?

As far as I'm concerned, the ship for great sitcoms sailed when *Friends* was cancelled. It's possible that some of you are too young to know the plot of every episode of *Friends* like those of us who came of age in the nineties (pity). So, I'll offer a quick summary.

Six friends enjoy life together in the Big Apple. Rachel and Monica live together in an adorable apartment that must have cost approximately a bajillion dollars at New York City rates. But apparently it was rent controlled because the girls could afford it on Rachel's tips as a waitress-turned-Ralph Lauren fashion designer (because *that* happens!) and Monica's wages as a sometimes working (mostly not) chef. Chandler and Joey lived across the hall. Joey was a barely employed soap opera actor. No one could ever figure out what Chandler did for a living, but he must have had a clueless boss because he was always available to hang out across the hall.

Phoebe was an earthy hippie (and therefore my favorite character) who must have lived in an apartment close by because she was also free to get together all hours of the day. Ross was the only one with a real job. He was a pale-ontologist, but that didn't keep him from meeting up with the gang at Central Perk for a cup of coffee often.

The group got along swimmingly, knew each other intimately, and kept each other tethered in the big city. They made us all wish we had friends like that.

There's a reason that *Friends* doesn't qualify for reality TV. It's because it's not reality.

Meeting up with people isn't effortless. Nurturing relationships doesn't fit easily into our jam-packed schedules and busy lives. Conflicts aren't resolved in a thirty-minute slot. Finding true, deep connection isn't always fun, comfortable, or convenient.

Back to the Garden

Let's head back to the Garden again for a moment, shall we? In Genesis 3:9–13 we get a picture of how relationships really work without scripts:

> But the LORD God called to the man and said to him, "Where are you?" And he said, "I heard the sound of you in the garden, and I was afraid, because I was naked, and I hid myself." He said,

"Who told you that you were naked? Have you eaten of the tree of which I commanded you not to eat?" The man said, "The woman whom you gave to be with me, she gave me the fruit of the tree, and I ate." Then the LORD God said to the woman, "What is this that you have done?" The woman said, "The serpent deceived me, and I ate."

Looks like real life is more like a soap opera than an episode of *Friends*. Our natural bent is to sabotage our relationships. Our tendency is to blame and to quarrel and to distance ourselves. When Eve took a nibble of that forbidden fruit, she sealed the fates of all of us. Relationships would be messy as a result of sin from that point forward.

Some of the ladies we interviewed for this book could be poster children for messiness. Katelyn feels lonely because she is still learning how to forge deep relationships. Becky admits she has huge walls up as a result of past pain. Andrea is anxious because being known requires vulnerability and that makes her uncomfortable. Angel is an introvert who struggles to have the bravery required to get to know others.

Others faced lonely seasons as a result of their circumstances. Kailey says she's been lonely most of her life because she has a hard time adapting to change. Melissa became lonely after a divorce. Amy faced loneliness when her child got sick and then again when the bottom fell out of her family's finances. Stephanie has a daughter with crippling anger and anxiety. The family stays close to home to avoid meltdowns and as a result Stephanie feels isolated and alone.

> We all have to choose if we want to hold on to the familiar pain of loneliness or do the very heavy lifting required to be known. #connected

Some of these women faced loneliness as a bump in the road. Others got stuck there. Their lives teach us an important lesson—how we respond to our circumstances, our pain, our sin, and the harsh reality of this fallen world will determine if loneliness visits for a season or unpacks its bags to stay. Neither option is easy. We all have to choose if we want to hold on to the familiar pain of loneliness or do the very heavy lifting required to be known.

Making Peace with Messy

Christa knows all about this choice. She has buried two babies. The first lived until he was five. He was a sick child and Christa spent her days and nights caring for him. That led to a season of isolation as a side effect of the need to protect him from the outside world. Several years and three more children later Christa and her husband had another sick baby.

"But the fifth arrived, and though he was declared healthy, we soon found out that he wasn't," she said. "We had to divide and conquer, so I was lonely in the hospital room with the baby who might not make it, and my husband was lonely at home with three boys who would never stop moving. During the days, I was still lonely at the hospital, and my husband was lonely at the office.

"Then the night came when I called him at 3:00 a.m. to tell him that we had to plan another burial, and who could stay with the boys while he came now to the hospital because loneliness was breaking me in the midst of the business of the PICU. He woke a neighbor and came heartbroken. We cried, we grieved, we decided to survive."

Christa is surviving but she admits that her pain has changed the way she approaches relationships. She feels uncomfortable around new people because she doesn't know how to explain what has happened and hates the pity they often offer. The world feels particularly unsafe to her because she never knows when someone might accidentally pick the scab of her grief, forcing her to feel it all over again.

Loneliness and pain seem to be two sides of the same coin. When we are hurting, we often feel the most alone because no one can grieve for us. We want someone to take it away and if they cannot, we feel like the hurt must be carried alone.

Stephanie knows all about that. After a big move and a destroyed friendship, she battled loneliness because it felt like no one could help heal her wounds.

"I tried Facebook," she told us. "I logged off within a couple of days. I needed to cry with someone. I needed to have someone help me feed my toddler as I sat and breastfed. I needed someone to tell me a joke so I could get my mind off my shattered friendships. I was tired of having to pretend when I was around actual people, like in Walmart or church, that I was sane, normal, holding it together."

There's no doubt that these women faced desperate circumstances. I want to be careful about assigning blame or acting like if they just made a little more effort to get to know others, loneliness would have receded out of their lives. That's an oversimplification. But these women did exactly what Adam and Eve did in the Garden. When things went haywire, they decided to hide.

Hiding may seem easier at the onset. Sharing our pain with others is difficult, awkward, and often disappointing. And yet, God's Word gives us this advice: "Bear one another's burdens, and so fulfill the law of Christ" (Gal. 6:2).

What does Paul mean when he says that bearing each other's pain fulfills Christ's law? In Matthew 22:39 Jesus says that the second greatest commandment is that we love our neighbors as ourselves. We think love is candy hearts and warm fuzzy feelings, but God's definition of love is much messier than our Hallmark version.

God didn't let Adam and Eve stay hidden. He came and found them and compassionately clothed them. They argued and deflected blame. It wasn't a feel-good conversation. Yet, God chose to enter the mess. In the same way, Jesus is the ultimate burden bearer. He took our greatest burden, sin, upon Himself on the cross and then asks us to bring the rest of our junk to Him to carry (1 Pet. 5:7). He sets an example for us in this way. When we help carry the pain of others, we imitate Him and when we let others into our pain, our sin, and our mess we give them opportunities to do the same.

In fact, the Bible is chock-full of examples of messy relationships. God and His "on-again, off-again" love affair with the Israelites comes to mind. (Keeping in mind that the "off-again" part was always from the Israelites. God's love for them was steadfast!)

Jesus' patient friendship with disciples who tended to mess things up is another example. The epitome of this principle is the story of Hosea and Gomer found in the Old Testament book of Hosea. Hosea's wife was a cheating, scheming, wayward woman. And yet, God's repeated instructions were for Hosea to be reconciled to her. Just like Adam and Eve, our default is to mess things up and yet God's Word seems to press us toward preserving relationship even when the cost is high.

If you're going to get connected, you're going to have to make peace with messy relationships. You're going to have to be okay with letting others in when you are at your worst and your life is a total train wreck. You also must be willing to turn the tables. When other people's lives are messy, you can't turn a blind eye or offer cheap words of comfort. You must willingly walk into the mess, even if they're hiding, and bear the bad stuff together.

> If you're going to get connected, you're going to have to make peace with messy relationships. #connected

I learned this lesson in a high school library recently. Two sixteen-year-old girls had been killed in a car accident in the small town where I live. Because I work with teenagers often, I was invited to come to the school as a grief counselor.

When I stepped through the doors, the pain was palpable. Teenagers aren't good at hiding their emotions. I love that about them. They weren't politely crying into their hankies. They were sobbing. It was ugly and awkward and hard to watch.

As I sat at a table taking it all in, I was struck by the fact that God meets us so intimately in our pain. In fact, He walks headlong into it. The Bible says that He's close to us when we're brokenhearted (Ps. 34:18). When we are weary and fed up, He wants us to come to Him (Matt. 11:28). The teenagers I saw modeled His example that day. They didn't hide their hurt from each other. They didn't put on a brave face. They willingly walked into each other's messy pain. As a result, they faced an extremely difficult time in community, not alone.

Hear me. If you don't want to be lonely, you must be willing to be messy.

The Bad By-Product of Convenience

Being a burden bearer is not the only example Christ sets for us in our relationships. You don't have to be hiding major pain to be missing His mark. For those of us who are experiencing smooth sailing for the moment, loneliness can come into our lives as a by-product of our refusal to be inconvenienced just as easily as it comes from our refusal to get messy.

I suspected that our culture's worship of all things convenient was playing a role in the pandemic of loneliness, so I came up with another social experiment. I decided to give up everything automated for one whole month.

The rules were simple:

No automated anything.

No ATMs.

No pay at the pump.

No online bill pay.

Because I learn best through total submersion, I intentionally chose a month when I had an exceptional amount of travel booked. With three speaking engagements and some media stops, I had fourteen flights booked in twenty-four days.

When the first day of the month hit, I packed up to head out on a trip to Alabama. As I drove to the airport it occurred to me that automatic kiosks for checking in and printing boarding passes were out. I would actually have to talk to airline employees. Um . . . have you noticed that airline employees can be a little, shall we say, snarky? I started to panic. Maybe I couldn't hack life without machines.

At the parking garage, I struck up a conversation with my shuttle driver. You should know I would never have done this before. I am a strictly head down traveler. No unnecessary conversation. No eye contact ever. To be honest, I am also often a lonely traveler. Believe it or not, it never occurred to me that the two might be connected.

On my flight I decided to actually talk to my seatmates. I felt a wave of nausea as I asked, "So . . . where ya headed?" I wasn't sure if it was motion sickness or nerves from talking to a stranger, so I kept talking.

Turns out the guy next to me was heading to St. Louis for business. He's a financial consultant from Georgia with a seven-year-old daughter he adores. It also turns out that airplane chatter can be contagious. The girl next to him jumped right in. She is a pathologist who was heading in from a convention in Baltimore. She's super passionate about tissue samples and her new husband. The three of us chatted the entire flight.

At one point I got up to head to the lavatory (code for tiny, yucky potty on plane). It was twenty rows back.

As I walked I took stock of my fellow travelers. None of them were talking. Most of them had their noses buried in a Kindle, iPad, or iPhone. Some were asleep. But for twenty rows, there was total silence. Silence can be golden, but it rarely accompanies connection.

When I returned to my seat, the conversation started flowing easily again with the people in my row. We were the only three people talking on the entire flight.

Often on such trips, I find myself tightly wrapped in the familiar pangs of loneliness. I am a girl traveling alone and the bigness of the world smacks me in the face. Many times I've found myself staring out the window wondering about my own significance in a world so big.

But not on that flight. On that flight I felt connected. Before I knew it we were touching down and the financial consultant, the pathologist, and I walked together to the baggage claim. I was no longer in a crowd of strangers. I was a part of a band of friends.

But then . . . I had to get my car out of parking.

I always choose the automated lane. It's fast and easy and I can just swipe my card and go. No connection necessary. I felt that small pang of panic that was becoming familiar as I realized I would have to choose the booth with an actual person in it this time.

Strangely, the automated option had a line four cars long. The human being option? It was vacant. It occurred to me in that moment that loneliness is convenient. Connection is not. We love convenience so much that we are willing to accept lonely lines and lonely trips and lonely lives.

We think of loneliness as something that is inflicted upon us but it turns out in areas like convenience and technology, we are inflicting the pain on ourselves.

That night at the airport, I chose to connect. I actually talked to the attendant while the cars next to me simply swiped their credit cards and drove away. She was sweet and helpful. She even asked if I had a coupon. I did! I had forgotten all about it.

On that trip alone my willingness to forgo convenience, to slow down, and to look other people in the eye won me two new friends and a 20 percent discount. Not bad!

Fast-forward forty-eight hours and I found myself on the road again. This time I was sitting in the airport in Denver. I am a slow learner, so I defaulted to my tendency to sit alone and look intently at my iPhone, lest anyone consider striking up a conversation.

I had left my family behind through tears that morning. My littlest one was sick and I was road weary. I didn't want to be alone in the world. I wanted to hole up with my family and tend to the ones who know me well.

I suppose I could have carried that loneliness with me for the entire trip. I would have too, except for an extroverted guy who sat down next to me and started talking. For the first few minutes I acted like my in-box contained the biggest secrets of humanity. I stared intently and tried to give off the cool traveler/I-don't-want-to-talk-to-you vibe. But he kept talking. Turns out that he and his wife had just separated and he was forced to leave behind his four-month-old daughter in order to start a brand new life on his own.

Maybe my morning hadn't been so rough after all. Connecting with others has a way of giving us perspective.

We chatted for a long time. I've become so used to isolation that connection kinda scares me. My tendency in these situations is to think something shady is going down. Maybe this guy was using the worst pickup line of all time (Uh . . . I just left my wife and baby daughter. Wanna grab a burger?). But it wasn't like that. We were just two people on separate treks who turned and looked at each other for a minute or two. We shared our stories and pictures of our kids. And in the middle of a huge airport, in a huge city, in a huge world, for a moment the loneliness eased.

The connections I found during my month without automation were refreshing and life giving, but they certainly weren't convenient.

Google It

If we were to build an altar to our worship of convenience, I think it might be sponsored by Google.

Close your eyes for a moment and try to imagine life without Google. What would you do if you needed to know how to make a pie crust? You would have to call your momma. What if some new friends from church invited you over for dinner? How would you know how to get there? You would pick up a phone and ask. What if you wanted to learn how to garden, or how to build a treehouse, or how to paint with watercolors? You would have to take a class, ask an expert, or at the very least enter a bookstore (remember those?). You would be unable to learn how to do things by watching a YouTube video or reading an answer from Ask.com. Human contact would be required to solve basic, everyday problems.

Instead, as a society we have removed the need for connection. Our iPhones know everything, so there's no need to ask questions of others. But what if convenience isn't as great as we all think it is? Is it possible that inconvenience is the real sweet spot?

An Inconvenienced God

As I read the Gospels, one fact is undeniable to me—Jesus valued people. Over and over He allowed Himself to be stopped, inconvenienced, and used by the people around Him.

There was the time He retreated to a mountain hideout for some much-needed rest only to be chased down by a crowd of needy seekers. What did Jesus do? He healed them. Then there was the time He was literally on His way to heal a sick girl when another woman grabbed His robe and got His attention. He stopped and tended to her need. There was the time He went way out of His way to heal a demon-possessed man that others saw as a lost cause. Oh, and there were the children Jesus urged to come to Him even though they seemed to pull Him away from His many ministry responsibilities.

As I study the book of Matthew I am dumbfounded by Jesus' patience for inconveniences. The entire book reads like a string of interruptions to His life. Everywhere He went people stopped Him, asked Him for His attention, and sought to redirect His path.

To be honest, the fact that Jesus always seemed to make time for others doesn't always sit well with me. That's because valuing people isn't one of my strong suits. I tend to elevate tasks and schedules and crossing items off of my to-do lists. These things fit nicely into the boxes I draw for how I want my life to look. In contrast, valuing people requires much of my time and energy. It's often messy. It rarely sticks to a schedule. I may be more Type A (I often call myself Type AA) than most, but our society trains each of us to value schedules and accomplishments more than people. Perhaps it's worth considering that the payoff for exchanging tasks for relationships is not what we anticipated.

Valuing people means adopting an overt willingness to be inconvenienced. It means doing things that cannot be measured. It means developing relationships based on who people really are and not who we want them to be.

My husband and I host a small group in our home.

> Valuing people means adopting an overt willingness to be inconvenienced. It means doing things that cannot be measured. #connected

That group has become one of my greatest insulators against loneliness. We truly bear each other's burdens on a regular basis. We pray for each other. We cry together. We bring meals when someone is sick or a new baby arrives. We share fears, and doubts, and lawn mowers.

It is the best example of the New Testament church that I've ever known.

But let me be clear, it is not convenient.

Meeting together regularly interrupts our schedules. It interferes with extracurricular activities and bed times. It takes effort to care for each other. Needs rarely pop up on weekends and evenings. But that's what valuing people looks like. It means accepting a dirty house because people have been loved, cared for, and entertained within the walls of your home. It means accepting a schedule in flux because you are determined to make time for others whenever necessary. It means considering the tasks on your to-do list as less important than the people you're doing them for. It means measuring success through relationships—not how neat and tidy your life looks.

Being known won't fit onto a checklist and it won't be convenient. Christian community has become a buzzword for something we do, something we can put into our day planner, but that's not true community.

Jesus knew all about this. His community was no cakewalk. Judas betrayed Him. Peter denied Him. Paul persecuted His flock and yet . . . Jesus pursued a relationship with them.

If you want to be known you must be willing to get messy and you've got to ditch the idol of convenience our culture worships so freely. I'm shooting you straight because I want you to know it's not an easy road. But it is one that God has always walked, and it leads to a life more meaningful and connected than any sitcom writer could ever dream of.

CHAPTER 7

The Secrets of the Wholehearted

Murphy's Law says that anything that can go wrong typically will go wrong. Oh, Murphy. How right you are.

I can think of a time several years ago when Murphy's Law was in full effect at my house. I was working on a really tight writing deadline. There was no room in my schedule for unplanned interruptions. Apparently, the nasty staph infection that invaded my husband's hand didn't get the memo.

I was trying to write with one hand and wrangle my small children with the other when the phone rang. My husband was at the doctor and called with the news that a wound we had dismissed as a bug bite was actually an infection caused by a strain of staph that does not respond well to medicine. The doctors were considering admitting him. They were almost certain he would permanently lose the use of his hand. They also said there was a 10 percent chance he wouldn't survive the infection at all. It was one of those moments where time seems to freeze and fear stands at your front door and knocks. I wanted to pray but I couldn't get words past the lump in my throat. I feared for the wellbeing of my man, I had to care for my kiddos, and I was anxious about meeting my deadline.

At that moment a friend called and I broke down. She prayed with me and asked if she could recruit others to pray. I didn't want to sound rude, so I said okay. She kept her word. Within a few hours tons of people were praying for our family. They called and texted with encouraging Scripture or by simply saying "we're praying."

Here's the funny thing. All of that prayer didn't make me feel better. At least not at first. The emotion that I felt the strongest that afternoon was embarrassment. I didn't like everyone knowing that things weren't perfect behind our front door. I didn't like the feeling that I couldn't pray myself out of this mess all on my own. Most of all, I didn't like the harsh reality that I couldn't keep all the plates spinning perfectly.

In that moment, I was in the epicenter of what a strong community is supposed to be like. I had people around me who were concerned for me and wanted to help, but there was something very specific required from me—vulnerability. I was vulnerable in this instance, but only under duress. If I had a choice, I would have opted to maintain a façade and handle the crisis alone rather than get real and let others in.

It is no coincidence that my aversion to vulnerability ran parallel to my deep feelings of loneliness.

The Secrets of the Wholehearted

Brené Brown is a research professor. Her particular niche of study happens to be vulnerability. In fact, she has spent an entire decade studying the way vulnerability impacts relationships. The fact that the topic warrants such extensive study indicates that I'm not the only one with big issues about getting real. I want to borrow from Brené heavily for a bit here, because I think her research is so groundbreaking and insightful.

Ten years of studying human connectedness led Brené to lump us all into one of two groups. There are those with a strong sense of love and belonging. This is the team we all want to be on. This is the group we all want to hang with. But as we've seen, this team can be elite and elusive. Being among the truly connected doesn't come easily.

Brené identified the second group as those who struggle for connection. They're always wondering if they're good enough. These are the lonely ones among us who are left sitting on the bench and watching others play ball.

Brené labeled those who were connected as being "wholehearted." The things the wholehearted group had in common hold the secrets to our plan to vaccinate ourselves and others from the pandemic of loneliness. Here's what Brené found in the connected group:

Courage

Brown defined courage as the ability to tell the story of who you are with your whole heart. (Hence the label wholehearted.) "These folks had, very simply, the courage to be imperfect," Brené said.[1]

> Loneliness fades away when we are willing to live messy lives. True connection is a byproduct of our willingness to be imperfect. #connected

Are you noticing a theme? Isolation dissipates when we get real about our sin. Loneliness fades away when we are willing to live messy lives. True connection is a by-product of our willingness to be imperfect.

Think back to the way my friends and church rallied around me when my husband was ill. They took care of me. They prayed for me. They walked with me through a difficult trial. That's what we all want, isn't it? We want a cheering section. We want people who won't shy away when the going gets tough. We want support. But there is a cost. If we are going to be lumped among the wholehearted, we must be willing to be imperfect.

Compassion

The research showed that those who were connected had compassion toward themselves first and then others.[2] How do you have compassion for yourself? You don't get your proverbial underwear in a wad when you can't do/be/act perfect.

Have you picked up that I have some firstborn, Type A, all-American girl achievement hang-ups? Oh sure, I can hammer out a to-do list like a boss. Give me a task and I will kick it into next week. But relationships? Meh. Not so much my strong suit.

You're not a therapist, so I don't expect you to peel back all of the layers of my junk, but you've helped me more than you know. Writing this book about connection has thrown one thing in my face—I am my harshest critic. If I fail, struggle, or don't measure up to my expectations, I become my own punching bag. I suppose this is the antithesis to what Brené means when she asserts that the truly connected demonstrate compassion toward themselves.[3] Why does it work out that way?

Because if we won't allow ourselves to be imperfect, we certainly won't allow others to see the real us.

Vulnerability

The wholehearted group in Brené's study fully embraced vulnerability. That doesn't mean that it came easily or naturally to them. They simply surrendered to its necessity. In contrast, those who were disconnected talked about vulnerability as being excruciatingly painful.

Brené noted that the research seemed to indicate that vulnerability was at the core of shame and fear and our struggle for worthiness and yet it also seemed to show that vulnerability was the birthplace of joy, creativity, and belonging.[4]

This is the point in the book where you need to bust out your highlighter.

Vulnerability is the birthplace of belonging.

This is an area of our lives where so many of us need a rebirth.

No Partial Paralysis

Brené noticed our collective tendency to try to numb our vulnerability.

"We live in a vulnerable world," she said. "And one of the ways we deal with it is we numb vulnerability."[5]

But she also noticed that it is impossible for us to selectively numb our emotions. When we numb vulnerability, the other side of our heart is equally paralyzed.[6] We may not want to be vulnerable, but then we shouldn't expect to be connected. We may avoid showing our imperfections, but then we cannot expect others to show us who they really are. We may never get real, but we will end up isolated.

This tug-of-war reminds me of Becky. Becky came to one of our focus groups for this book. She's in her thirties and readily admits that she has had a lifelong struggle with loneliness. Not surprisingly, she's also afraid to be vulnerable.

"I really care what people think about me," Becky said. "So I believe that if I'm totally myself, people will leave."

Here's the inside scoop. Becky had to be dragged, nearly kicking and screaming to the interview. She used every excuse she could think of to get out of it. It was only because of a persistent friend who wouldn't let her off the hook that we heard Becky's story at all.

When we pressed her on this she said that she didn't want to get real because she didn't want to seem weak. There's a name for that. It's pride.

You see, pride is the yin to vulnerability's yang. What is pride exactly? It's preserving the image of perfection. It is an attempt (however futile) to spackle over the cracks in our lives in an attempt to appear flawless.

It Cometh before a Fall

The Bible has plenty to say about pride and none of it is an endorsement.

Perhaps the most famous pride verse is Proverbs 16:18 which says, "Pride goes before destruction, and a haughty spirit before a fall."

Pride won't bring anything beautiful into our lives. If you are determined to hold on to pride and attempt to spin your imperfections, you can be assured you'll fall flat on your face.

Why does pride push us toward a fall? Because it is rooted in three dangerous lies.

Lie #1: I am autonomous.

Autonomy is the sense that you are self-governing. It's the idea that you're an independent being with the right to do whatever you want. The mantra of our autonomous self screams, "I'm in charge of me!"

It's all very "American dream," but it doesn't really jibe with what God's Word teaches.

Proverbs 3:5–6 asks us to acknowledge God in everything we do and let Him direct our paths. In Matthew

16:24–27, Jesus says that part of being a follower of Him is denying ourselves and laying down the lives we want for the life He has planned for us. James 4:7 presents willing submission to Christ as a way to preserve unity in our relationships with others.

John 3:30 puts it this way: "He must increase, but I must decrease."

The idea that you've been given the right to do what you want and run your own life doesn't fit into the formula for the way God asks us to live as Christ followers.

If we've been in church for a while, we've learned enough Christianese to know we are not supposed to arch our backs and scream, "I'm in charge of me!" But pride rears its ugly head and wriggles its way into our relationships and tells us to distance ourselves from community because it will inevitably limit our freedom and choice. If we allow ourselves to be truly connected to others, we won't have free rein over our own decisions anymore. Our fear of losing our autonomy often keeps us isolated and disconnected.

Lie #2: I am self-sufficient.

If autonomy is the notion that you are in charge, self-sufficiency is the idea that you can take care of yourself. It is our self-sufficient selves that are so resistant to depending on others. It's the self-sufficient side of pride that makes it so hard to admit our shortcomings and confess our sins. Our belief that we can take care of things on our own makes us avoid reaching out for help because we want to try to fix things all on our own.

The harsh reality is that you are not able to fix what is broken in your life.

Can you change the habits that wreak havoc in your relationships? Not on your own, or you would have by now. Can you break the power of sin in your life? The fact that you can't is what the gospel is all about. (We'll chase that rabbit all the way down the trail in chapter 11.) Can you keep death at bay? Heal yourself when you're sick? Do something about the variables of this world that make you afraid? No. You can't. It doesn't take much to pop the bubble that we can handle everything on our own. We are small and weak in a big, strong world. Most of us spend our days in denial of this truth. That only keeps us from pressing into one of the biggest gifts God has to give. Paul didn't make this mistake.

In 2 Corinthians 12:9 Paul wrote, "But he said to me, 'My grace is sufficient for you, for my power is made perfect in weakness,' Therefore I will boast all the more gladly of my weaknesses, so that the power of Christ may rest upon me.'"

To maximize connection with God and others, a simple flip is required. Nope, you can't fix things on your own, but God can. One of the ways He wants to provide for you is with a community of believers who can make up your slack.

Lie #3: I am sovereign.

Pride isn't always about keeping a mask on. Often there's a deeper, darker element at play.

Psalm 10:4 says, "In the pride of his face the wicked does not seek him, all his thoughts are "there is no God."

What does knowing there's a God have to do with our pride problem?

Only God is perfect. If pride is an effort to maintain the illusion of perfection, it's also an indication that we want to sit on the throne. We prefer the worship of others instead of connection to them. We'd rather be adored than be known.

Humility is required to love and be loved as your authentic self. Pride fights for fake relationships built on hollow praise.

> Humility is required
> to love and be
> loved as your
> authentic self.
> #connected

A Vulnerable Faith

Our struggle for sovereignty is a big part of the reason why God warns us so strongly against pride in His Word. It is a barrier between us and Him.

Pride says, "I don't need You, God." It whispers, "I can do this on my own." That's pride's arrogant side. But pride can be schizophrenic. The insecure side of pride tells us to pull an Adam and Eve, to hide from God because if He really knew us, He would disapprove.

We know that God sees us completely. We can read in His Word that there really is no hiding from Him, and yet, we still try to come to Him all wrapped up in a perfect bow. Our prayers are shallow and filled with Christian catchphrases instead of gut-wrenchingly honest confessions about our deep flaws and needs.

Adam and Eve were unwillingly vulnerable. Suddenly sideswiped by their own imperfections, they ran into the bushes to hide. God was not surprised by their imperfections. He went looking for them in their messed up state and seized the opportunity to lovingly connect. Chances are, if you're not vulnerable with the people in your world, you may be hiding (or rather attempting to hide) the real you from God too.

When we try to build a relationship with the Lord on the same projection of false perfection we use with our friends and family, we get the same result—distance, isolation, and loneliness. The poster children for this reality would be the Israelites. If God and His people could list their relationship status in the Old Testament, it would definitely say, "It's complicated." Due to the Israelites' cycle of rebellion, their relationship with God was on-again, off-again. No doubt, this led to seasons of distance and isolation. But that was never God's choice. He does not change. He does not retreat from us. When distance and isolation creep into our relationship with Him, it is always our choice, not God's.

I've said all along that the answer to our loneliness is twofold. Just like Adam, we are hardwired for intimacy with each other *and* we are hardwired for intimacy with the Lord. Both require us to be vulnerable and to open-handedly display how broken we truly are.

There are lots and lots (and lots) of warnings against pride in the Bible. With so many warnings, we would do well to take heed. But what if the punishment for pride isn't fire and brimstone, but a lonely life? What if the fall the psalmist predicted is descriptive of the kind of life that comes when we exhaust our energy preserving the image of perfection? What if vulnerability is the secret to escaping the inevitable land mines of life with minimal harm?

Yes, it's true that vulnerability can be painful. There are times when it makes it feel like we are at the helm of a sinking ship. But when it comes to connectedness to God and others, it seems that vulnerability is also our life raft.

The Confession that Saved My Life

Flash back with me to another time when Murphy's Law was wreaking havoc on my life. I had just had my second baby and was totally knocked off-kilter by postpartum depression.

I've written about it before in other books, but I've never been willing to say how bad things got. Since this is a chapter about vulnerability, I reckon it's time to rip that Band-Aid off. I had the crying and anxiety that often comes with the baby blues, but there was something else at work in my hormone-crazed mind. For the first time ever, I was thinking about ending my own life.

Even as I write those words it seems crazy. I wasn't exactly suicidal in the traditional sense. I wasn't depressed. But for me postpartum depression led to racing, irrational thoughts. One of which, was imagining myself taking my own life. It was a graphic image that seemed to crash into my mind several times a day.

That's not pretty stuff. A perfect Christian and a perfect mom would certainly never struggle with something so dark. I didn't want to tell anyone. But I had learned the lesson my husband's staph infection had the power to teach. I could keep my secret under wraps but the cost would be isolation and loneliness. Or I could get real and tell someone. That choice would be painful too, but it was the only way to avoid walking through the fire alone.

And so . . . I told. I told a group of other moms what was going on inside my head. It took courage, certainly. To borrow Brené's definition, telling my story with my whole heart, and not just the parts that looked pretty, was scary. It required compassion. I had to let myself off the massive hook I was hanging from. It took vulnerability. I had to smash the mask of perfection on the ground and let people see the real me underneath. But what I found was connection, grace, kindness, and a group of women who were willing to carry me through that time. This could have been one of the loneliest times in my life and instead it was one of the richest relationally. Go figure.

Who knows how the story would have ended if I had insisted on preserving the image of perfection. I'm afraid that with pride there are no happy endings.

Jesus made a similar confession when He found Himself at a painful crossroads. He and His disciples had just finished the last supper. Knowing that His arrest, trial, and crucifixion were right around the corner, Jesus chose to press into His community. For some reason, I've always sort of imagined that the last supper was some sort of favor to the disciples, that maybe Jesus would have preferred to spend His last night alone, but if we fast-forward just a few verses, we see that this isn't true.

After Jesus ate and sang with His disciples, they moved out to the Garden of Gethsemane. In this familiar scene, we see Jesus demonstrate what vulnerability really looks like.

Matthew 26:38 says, "Then he said to them, 'My soul is very sorrowful, even to death; remain here, and watch with me.'"

Jesus wasn't stoic. He didn't slap on a brave face. He said, "I am sad to the point it feels like dying."

That's really what I was trying to say to my mom friends. "I'm sad. I'm struggling. The life feels like it's being squeezed out of me." I didn't realize it at the time but when I got real about my pain, I was imitating Christ.

Jesus was fully God and fully man. He didn't experience weakness at the level that the rest of us do, but in this moment He chose not to take care of everything Himself. He chose to defer to the sovereignty of His Father. He chose to get real and to press into the friends that surrounded Him. He chose not to face His darkest moments alone. We'd do well to follow His lead.

Woe to Me!

Jesus is not the only example of vulnerability in the Bible. The prophet Isaiah's prayer found in Isaiah 6 is one of the most vulnerable prayers in the entire Bible. After seeing God on His throne, Isaiah uttered these words: "Woe is me! For I am lost; for I am a man of unclean lips, and I dwell in the midst of a people of unclean lips; for my eyes have seen the King, the LORD of hosts!" (Isa. 6:5).

Let me give a modern paraphrase: "I'm a hot mess. I will never get my act together, no matter how hard I try. Oh, and the rest of the world? It's totally messed up too. None of us are even close to perfect. Seeing how perfect God is only exposes how messed up and weak we really are."

No spackle there.

Isaiah didn't try to gloss over his imperfections. He didn't spin his culture or justify his failures. There was no pride in Isaiah's heart in that moment. He was painfully aware of his shortcomings. Preserving the image of perfection was not an option.

And what was the result? He got to see God. He was with the Lord in the throne room. He had an intimate conversation with Him about the things that were to come.

A prideful man would not have been granted such a privilege. Someone bent on appearing perfect would almost certainly miss the wonder of the flawlessness of God.

The Big Secret

Maybe your man doesn't have a raging staph infection. You might not have postpartum depression . . . but there's something that you don't want told. There's a part of you that you want to keep deeply hidden. Pride tells you to "Shut up" because no one will accept you. But vulnerability whispers the quiet truth, "Stop trying to convince them you're perfect. No one is buying it anyway."

Maybe like Becky, you're sure that if the truth got out about who you really are, others would see you as weak. But here's a secret we all need unlocked. Weakness is universal. It's the reason we need each other and the reason we need a relationship with such a strong God.

Do you want an intimate relationship with

> Weakness is universal. It's the reason we need each other and the reason we need a relationship with such a strong God. #connected

God? Stop coming to Him scrubbed clean. Don't try to convince Him you're perfect, but tell Him how needy you really are. Don't approach Him thinking "look at me," but rather "woe is me" and watch the walls between you crumble.

Do you find intimate connection with other people to be elusive? Perhaps you've been spackling over the parts of you that others will be most drawn to. If you want to be lumped among the wholehearted, you must have the courage to tell the story of who you really are.

CHAPTER 8

A Modern
Trojan Horse

After a fruitless ten-year war against the city of Troy, the Greeks come up with a strategy to secure their place in the annals of history. They construct a massive horse designed to hide an elite force of their best fighters. The rest of the Greek army sails off into the sunset, leaving their enemies to believe that they have given up the fight. Relieved that the conflict is finally over and assuming that the giant horse is an offering to the god Athena, the Trojans wheel the beast into the fortified walls of their city.

Night falls and the Greek special forces climb out of their hiding place and unlock the gates for their fellow soldiers who have returned under the cloak of darkness. Troy is destroyed. The war ends. The Greeks win.

No, this book hasn't taken a hard right turn into the subject of ancient mythology. We aren't delving into the study of movies with Brad Pitt and Orlando Bloom either. (Although let's face it, girls, that would be a very interesting read.) The topic at hand is still loneliness, but we need to revisit the story of the Trojan horse, because too many of us have pulled our own version of that horse into the gates of our lives.

For our purposes, a Trojan horse is simply this: Something we invite into our lives, thinking it's a gift, but in time it turns and attacks the things we most treasure.

We've already looked at some Trojan horses in this book. Technology can be a Trojan horse. So can perfection. But there's another idol that so many of us look to as a trophy of our success. We should pay close attention, because this gift may be our downfall.

This idol may not look like a giant horse. It's more likely to resemble your job or your church or your kids' sports schedule. In the war for true connectedness, the Trojan horse sitting outside our gates is busyness.

Here's a look at just how big this idol has become.

- One study found that 80 percent of Americans work the equivalent of a second workday *after* leaving the office.[1]
- We're doing plenty of work inside our office walls too. Nearly 10 million Americans worked more than 60 hours per week last year. We work longer hours than almost every other advanced country.[2]

- Fifty-seven percent of Americans have up to two weeks of unused vacation at the end of each year.[3]
- We're too busy to sleep. More than one-third of working Americans sleep less than six hours per night. That means there are 40 million of us suffering from chronic sleep deprivation.[4]
- One-third of us are living with 'extreme stress daily and half of us are regularly lying awake at night because of our stress.[5]

Yep, we're a busy bunch and our breakneck pace is hitting where it hurts.

Sacred Deprivation

Several years ago I found myself chronically exhausted. It seemed that no matter how often I went to bed early or how many naps I took, I just couldn't seem to shake my weariness. It was in that tired state that I had an epiphany. I wasn't worn out from a lack of sleep. I was tired from a lack of the sacred.

A synonym for *sacred* is *untouchable*. Suddenly it was clear to me. There was no part of my day that was untouchable to the demands of everyday life. Without regular moments of sacred, life started to whiz by at an unbearable pace.

Judging by the stats on our busyness, I bet I'm not the only one who has experienced sacred deprivation. One study found that 60 percent of Christians around the world feel that their hectic schedule prevents them from spending more time with God.[6] We may not say it out loud, but our schedules are sending this clear message: "Lord, I'm too busy for You." It's no wonder we're all feeling so disconnected.

"The times I've been lonely are when I am not connected with God, not keeping that relationship up," Dianne told us. She's in her fifties and an empty nester. "For me, it's been times when I am really busy and haven't taken the time to get into the Word, taken the time to really pray."

Dianne noticed a connection that many of us do not. When we let busyness crowd out the sacred, we get lonely. When we let our schedules crowd out God, we are left feeling desperately depleted.

Pulling the Ripcord

The first wave of emotions to hit me after the "seismic shift" I spoke of in the first chapter was loneliness. The second wave was the realization that I had been worshipping busyness for my entire adult life.

The Davises are not a couple particularly fond of gray areas. We tend to live in the extremes. We recognized our busyness was straining our relationships with God and others, so we pulled hard on the ripcord in an attempt to float into a simpler life. We sold our home in the city and bought a farm. As in, a real farm. With a barn, a herd of horses, and a fainting goat. We became residents of what I believe to be the last town in America without a Walmart. For the record, there's no Chick-fil-A or Target either. (That's not heresy. I checked.)

It was refreshing to trade in the sounds of sirens and traffic for crickets and the occasional coyote, but we also had to face the unromantic reality that came with stepping out of the rat race. Can I shoot you straight? It doesn't feel like a beach vacation, and there's an awful lot of manure to scoop. But walking away from our busyness has made a huge difference in our ability to connect. Our faith is richer and our family closer knit than it was when we were running at warp speed.

Farm livin' may not be the life for you. The good news is it doesn't have to be. But take it from someone who has waited an hour in your carpool line, it's time to stop the insanity. I looked into the crystal ball of my family's future and saw way too much busyness there. True, I got a little radical with my solution, but you don't have to. If you are reeling from overcommitment, overscheduling, and stretched-too-thin disease, let me assure you that it's possible to do something about it.

You already know the bad news. We are a culture totally ravaged by overcommitments. We all know it and we look at each other apologetically when we say things like, "I'm just *so* busy" or "The kids just have so much going on" while we simultaneously add more into our iPhones, complete with multiple reminders so we don't forget what's next.

The result is that many of us are desperate for quality time with the people we love the most. We wake up exhausted and go to bed exhausted, and our spirits limp along with no rest, no reflection, and very little time with our Rescuer. In a sermon on busyness, my pastor recently said that American families are going with the flow straight down the toilet. That'll preach.

Kailey told us that for her, busyness makes her feel disconnected. "I feel like I'm busy, but it's useless busyness. At the end of the day, I haven't really been with anyone, except maybe my husband for like thirty minutes. I'm not busy because I'm connected with people. I don't feel like I have time to build relationships with people."

The result of all that running and doing and scheduling is collective bone weariness. It should not surprise us that our relationships are shallow and unfulfilling. We have nothing to offer each other.

What Busyness Isn't

Let's pull the emergency brake for a moment and take a look at what busyness isn't.

Busyness is not productivity. Study after study has shown that all the working we are doing often just puts us on a hamster wheel. Just because you are working more does not actually mean that you are doing more.

Proverbs 14:4 says, "Where there are no oxen, the manger is clean, but abundant crops come by the strength of the ox."

Maybe it's the farm girl in me, but I just love it when the Lord uses livestock references. This little gem from Proverbs has much to teach us about the beauty of true productivity. The writer contrasts two images. The first is a barn without an ox. True, it's a clean barn. I can see how a clean barn might hold some appeal, especially considering the kind of yuck it might contain if an ox actually lived there. But barns aren't meant to be clean. They are meant to be used.

The second image includes the ox. What is the result of having an ox? According to this passage, it's abundant crops. Usefulness. Fruitfulness. Productivity!

Too many of us work for show. "Look how productive I am! Look how hard I work! Look how full my calendar is!" But we're just building an illusion. It's a clean barn. We're not really getting much done.

Work is good. The Bible esteems hard work. In fact, the Bible mentions the value of hard work somewhere in the neighborhood of thirty times. Sabbath rest (a concept we'll unpack more in a minute) is mentioned closer to a hundred and fifty times. It seems we have our wires crossed.

Productivity is good, but let me say it again—busyness is not productivity.

Busyness is also not indicative of your value. We all seem to have swallowed the Kool-Aid that we are busy because we are important (and we are important because we are busy). A nasty side effect is that we are embarrassed if we read a book cover to cover, spend an afternoon watching old movies or . . . (gasp!) take a nap.

At the beginning of summer, my husband ordered a hammock for each member of our family and anchored them to the poles on our back porch. His hammock is well loved. He's spent many afternoons resting there. My kids hang out in their hammocks too. But mine? I've never been in it. Not one single time. To spend an afternoon in a hammock would feel like an epic failure to me. What would I be contributing? How would I turn off the running to-do list in my mind? Make no mistake—my husband is not lazy. Neither are my children. They are not relaxing at times when there are more pressing matters, but they've made peace with downtime. I have watched out the kitchen window as they've swung together. They laugh. They talk. They enjoy each other's company. And I choose the dishes instead because I've taken the bait the culture has hurled at me that busyness equals value and fallen for the lie hook, line, and sinker.

If we're going to get un-lonely, we've got to stop the glorification of busy. We'll need to make a conscious effort not to have chaos. We'll have to get comfortable with a few blank pages in our day planner. We will have to write ourselves a big fat permission slip to lie in a hammock every once in a while.

> If we're going to get un-lonely, we've got to stop the glorification of busy. #connected

Calling a Colossal Time-Out

That image of my kiddos in their hammocks got me sidetracked. Since we are on the subject of busyness, let me zero in on fellow mommas for a minute.

I'm going to give it to you straight—when it comes to scheduling our families, we've all gone crazy. Let's use sports as an obvious example.

- In a study of sixteen declining congregations in the U.S. and Canada, the number one reason cited by clergy and church members for failing attendance was the "secularization of Sunday." Many church members cited their kids' sports as being the most critical factor.
- More than 1/3 of congregants in a separate study said school and sports-related activities was "quite a bit of an issue" when considering church attendance.
- About 2/3 of "Easter Christians" polled said they attend church only twice a year because they are too busy with other commitments including kids sports programs.[7]

Shouldn't someone throw the red flag here? Isn't it time we noticed that sports are pulling Christians out of the pews? There is bound to be a ripple effect. Church isn't just something we do. Church is the artery that pumps the necessary blood through our bodies to run the race of faith well. It can also be the birthplace for some of our deepest, most meaningful relationships.

Soccer games and baseball practices are not a good substitute.

I've spoken with several psychologists lately who treat children and adolescents. When I ask them what trends they are seeing, they all tell me the same thing—they've seen a massive influx in young patients dealing with anxiety. What's going on here? It seems our kiddos are suffering from secondhand stress. In one study of over one thousand 3rd–12th graders, an overwhelming majority of kids wished their parents would be less stressed out.[8] The pressure we are putting on our kids to be involved in every possible sport and activity while maintaining a perfect GPA and always keeping college admission in the back of their minds is messing them up. Remember that young people are fast becoming the loneliest demographic?

They may get into a Division I school on a football scholarship, but what good is it if they are desperately lonely?

Busyness is an idol that is attacking us indeed. And it is attacking our children.

Embracing the Paradox

It is not my intention to pack your bags for a guilt trip. I get that your schedule is a reflection of your genuine desire to do good for yourself and others. But let me go Dr. Phil on you for a moment: "How's that working for you?"

I know from experience, it probably isn't.

We cannot know and be known in the leftover slots on our calendar. We cannot have deep intimacy in the midst of constant chaos. We cannot nurture a relationship with God when there is no time for Him. So, how do we fix what we've broken?

Take a look at how Jesus did it.

Jesus spent time alone.

One of the pivotal moments of Jesus' ministry was the feeding of the five thousand, but the story has an odd ending: "Immediately Jesus made the disciples get into the boat and go on ahead of him to the other side, while he dismissed the crowd. After he had dismissed them, he went up on a mountainside by himself to pray" (Matt. 14:22–23 NIV).

Jesus had thousands of people waiting for Him and yet, He walked away. It wasn't as if His schedule suddenly cleared up and He had time to feed His spirit. I doubt the people just let Him go. He left when everyone was clamoring for more of Him. He took control of His schedule and figured out a way to be alone.

This was not a rare occurrence. In Matthew 13:1, we find Jesus sitting alone by a lake. In Matthew 15:29, He is sitting alone on the side of a mountain. In Luke 22:41, He pulled away from the pack of disciples to pray by Himself.

Luke 5:16 tells us that spending time alone was part of Jesus' usual rhythm. "But Jesus *often* withdrew to lonely places and prayed" (NIV, emphasis mine).

Jesus did not ask permission from others for quietness and solitude. Nor did He apologize for it. He took it because it was best for Him. It filled His tank with the fuel He needed to continue to pour into the lives of the people around Him. We should pay attention and follow His lead.

It's paradoxical that spending time alone can ease our loneliness, but God's way rarely jibes with the way we want to get things done. If we want to be less lonely, we must make time to be alone. It is extra critical that we make time to be alone with God. We've got to find a way to turn away from all that's on our plates and walk toward peace.

> We've got to find a way to turn away from all that's on our plates and walk toward peace. #connected

Psalm 46:10 is a well-worn verse, but perhaps it's become so familiar we've started to ignore it. "Be still, and know that I am God. I will be exalted among the nations, I will be exalted in the earth!"

Be. Still.

Slow down.

Tell the "to-do's" to take a chill pill. Because God is God and you are not.

If you don't get it all done, or make it to every church function, or have the planet's most well-rounded children, the world will keep spinning. Making it a priority to spend time alone and alone with the Father will fill you up. When you are full you are able to pour out. And when you pour out you are very likely to find yourself connected. Go figure.

Jesus honored the Sabbath.

When Jesus retreated from His usual pace, He was modeling the practice of Sabbath. Few subjects get as much real estate in the Bible as the Sabbath. A quick search turns up more than a hundred and fifty mentions of Sabbath rest beginning in Exodus and wrapping up in Hebrews. The concept of Sabbath literally bookends much of God's Word.

We first see the word *Sabbath* in Exodus 16:23. The Israelites had recently been delivered from the heavy hand of the Egyptians, and they were learning how to live in the wilderness. After telling them He would feed them with manna from heaven, God drops this commandment: "Tomorrow is a day of solemn rest, a holy Sabbath to the LORD."

We pick up two key parts of God's plan for Sabbath here. Sabbath is designed to be a day of solemn rest and Sabbath is holy.

This theme is woven through the rest of God's Word. In Exodus 20:8, Sabbath makes it into the Ten Commandments. Take notice that work, performance, and achievement did not. Can't we assume, then, that Sabbath is of paramount importance to God? You may be familiar with this commandment, but maybe it would do us some good to revisit it.

"Remember the Sabbath day, to keep it holy."

Notice what God isn't asking of us. He does not say, "Remember the Sabbath day, to keep it busy."

We associate Sabbath with the day we go to church. Certainly, a church service could be a valuable part of our Sabbath, but we tend to leave out the rhythm of space and rest that God modeled and then called us to emulate.

I know that's been true in our house. We've been involved in every church activity that we possibly could, resulting in a Sunday schedule that looked something like:

- Wake up exhausted
- Rush, rush, rush to get family fed, clothed, and out the door
- Yell at each other in the car
- Squeal into the parking lot
- March into church
- Rush through services, responsibilities, relationships with church members
- Race home
- Scarf down lunch
- Get ready for evening church
- Fall into bed exhausted
- Wait six days and repeat

I'll say it again: No wonder we're lonely. We are empty and tired and have nothing to give. The people around us are in the same state. We cannot nurture the intimacy with God and others that we are wired for at this pace.

Looks like we've found another fork in the road where we've collectively chosen the wrong path. God must have known we'd be slow learners in this area because He repeats His command to Sabbath over and over and over.

In Exodus 31:13, God commands the Israelites to keep His Sabbath day "above all." Clearly, when it comes to Sabbath rest, God means business.

In Leviticus 23:32, God commands Israel to keep Sabbath in observance of the Day of Atonement and His particular choice of words is telling: "It shall be to you a Sabbath of solemn rest, *and you shall afflict yourselves.* On the ninth day of the month beginning at evening, from evening to evening shall you keep your Sabbath" (emphasis mine).

The word *afflict* indicates that God gets that taking a day to rest and refuel requires self-denial. It is annoying to pull the brakes on our busyness. It's inconvenient to have a regular rhythm of rest. It goes against the grain to allow white space in our lives. God says to do it anyway.

The biblical prescription isn't all gloom and doom either. In Leviticus 26:34, God reminds us to enjoy His Sabbath. Mark 2:27 hammers this point home: "The Sabbath was made for man, not man for the Sabbath." The Sabbath is a gift to you. It's not something else you do. Not another check box for your to-do list. It certainly isn't a favor you offer to God. God asks us to honor the Sabbath because it's for our good. He hardwired us for connection, and then gave us a slot in which to connect.

For Jesus, Sabbath wasn't about rules or rigid scheduling. In Matthew 12, Jesus puts the Pharisees in their place when they tried to condemn Him and His disciples for eating grain together on the Sabbath. That same passage describes Jesus healing a man with a withered hand on the Sabbath. Sabbath isn't about shutting down and shutting others out. It's a space for connecting. If you have a chance to eat a meal with your friends, do it. If you can meet the needs of someone else, do that. Busyness chokes out these opportunities. Instead of being another box to check, Jesus shows us that part of Sabbath is making yourself available to be with and respond to others.

A Different Kind of Garden

We've spent plenty of time in Adam and Eve's garden in the pages of this book, but Eden isn't the only garden with relationship troubles. Can I take you on a quick tour of the plot in my backyard?

The month of May held so much promise. I tilled my soil, planted my seeds in neat little rows, and went to war against anything that looked like a weed. But as I write these words, it is early September and I've totally lost control. The green beans are entwined with some mystery vine. The tomatoes are in cahoots with pigweed. The corn has been taken over by some shady weeds that look like trouble. The leftover fruit is rotting on the vine.

When it comes to the state of my garden, the weeds aren't the real problem. They are simply the by-product of busyness. I've let other tasks yank me away from pulling weeds, harvesting ripe veggies, and tending to soil. The good stuff has been choked out by my tendency to get swept up in the tyranny of the urgent and forget to tend to the needs right under my nose. You don't have to be a gardener to make my mistake.

When it comes to relationships, we all want a spread in *Better Homes & Gardens*. We want things neat and tidy. We want rapid growth. We want an end result that delights and nourishes us. But we don't want to take time to simply sit and pull weeds. We're uncomfortable with the sometimes solitary work required to deal with potential invaders. We've run so fast and so hard for so long that we've gotten comfortable with weeds, but they're choking out the good stuff. We've got to recalibrate and find a way to make time for the sacred.

Sending the Trojan Horse Back

Allow me to rewrite history for a moment. After a ten-year war the Greeks retreat with no warning and leave in their place a giant wooden horse. The Trojans have a moment of clarity. They realize that this doesn't make sense. The jig is up. The small team of soldiers is easily defeated once exposed. Troy wins.

You can rewrite your own story, ya know? You don't have to keep pace with the rest of the world. Alone time is necessary. Sabbath is a command. Hammocks are not a sign of weakness.

Just like unplugging and embracing inconvenience, saying "no" to busyness will require you to go against the flow. The world isn't going to stop screaming for more of you. The myth that busy kids make better kids is unlikely to be debunked. But the way I see it, we can continue to allow our frenetic schedules to attack our relationships with God and others or we can decide to stop the madness.

If you decide to take control of your schedule, you can't expect everyone to just step in line. They're probably still looking at that Trojan horse as a gift. The clouds won't just part and provide an easy way for you to slow down. You've got to turn away from all that's on your plate and walk toward peace.

As a Christian, God deserves the firstfruits of your time and energy, not another excuse about why there's no time left to know and be known. As a parent, your children deserve to have the best of you, not the scraps left over by a bulging schedule. As someone with only one life to live, you deserve to know that rich relationships are possible. The world will keep on spinning. Our iStuff will keep on beeping. The offers to go and do and be will keep coming, but a peaceful life is possible and it's worth fighting for.

> God deserves the firstfruits of your time and energy, not another excuse about why there's no time left to know and be known. #connected

When it comes to your schedule, I'm praying you have a seismic shift of your own. If it comes with a fainting goat instead of a Trojan horse, well that's even better.

CHAPTER 9

The Golden Rule Is Tarnished

I still wish so badly that things had turned out differently.

My husband, Jason, and I took a thirteen-year-old foster son named Daniel into our home with the hopes of adopting him. We got to love him, pray with him, take him to school, and cook his dinner for almost a year. Then . . . he was gone. Some adoption stories end with pictures of a smiling family. Ours did not. Our boy went on to a different placement with a different family.

God has taken me through layers of learning in the wake of that loss. First, He gently bound up my wounds. That part of the process took years. I know firsthand how painful it can be to let your guard down. Once the bruises on my heart began to heal, God started to teach me a deeper lesson about my relationships—mainly that they are not about me. If I were to put everything I gave to Daniel on one side of a scale and everything he gave to me on another, the result would be way out of balance. But as I've thought about that relationship in the years since Daniel left, I've had the strong sense that Jesus wants me to ditch the scale altogether. Honestly, it's been a bitter pill to swallow.

I want relationships to work like an ATM. I give to others, and they spit out exactly what I request. Instead, it's more like a slot machine. I never know what I'm going to get in return, and sometimes I get nothing but X's across the board.

When our relationships result in disappointment, pain, rejection, or failure, most of us default to some version of withdrawal. The walls go up. Every time a relationship fails to meet our expectations, we add another layer of bricks. When the wall does what it's meant to do by keeping others out, we feel lonely, isolated, and left out. It's a vicious and painful cycle.

So, how do we change our ATM mentality? If our relationships aren't really about us, what are they really about?

Since we are called to be imitators of Christ (1 Cor. 11:1), perhaps the answers lie in Jesus' approach to relationships.

A Relational God

Pop quiz time. (Don't sweat it. I will give everyone an A for effort.)

Where do we first hear of Jesus in the Bible?

Are you thinking of Mary and the angel Gabriel? Sorry. *No bueno.* Did you maybe fast-forward a bit and think of tiny baby Jesus wrapped in swaddling clothes and lying in a manger? That's not it either. It was kind of a trick question. The first time Scripture mentions Jesus, it leaves out His name.

Check out Genesis 1:26: "Then God said, 'Let us make man in *our* image, after *our* likeness . . .'" (emphasis mine).

Who is God talking to here? Himself, actually. God the Father, God the Son, and God the Holy Spirit were present at creation. From the very first chapter of the very first book of the Bible we see God in the context of relationship. As we look at the Trinity throughout the Bible, we see that there is no fighting for the needs of the individual, but rather an intentional dependence. We see in the Triune God an example of relationships at their very best. As image bearers of God, we can

> As image bearers of God, we can know that we are also designed to live in community with others. #connected

know that we are also designed to live in community with others.

Jesus' relationships during His time on earth teach another important lesson about how we are to approach our own relationships. Let's take a quick flip through His Rolodex. (For you young things, that's a paper version of the contact list on your phone. Crazy. I know.)

Mary Magdalene

Mary Magdalene is very present throughout the Gospels. She often traveled with Jesus and the twelve disciples (Luke 8:1–2). She stayed right by Jesus' side through the crucifixion (John 19:25–26). She was the first person that He appeared to after His resurrection (John 20:14). We can assume that Jesus' relationship with Mary was an important one. She certainly offered love, support, and comfort to Jesus, but that's not how this relationship began.

Luke 8:2 describes Jesus' inner circle and says, "and also some women who had been healed of evil spirits and infirmities: Mary, called Magdalene, from whom seven demons had gone out."

Jesus didn't begin a relationship with Mary because she had something to offer Him. She was possessed by seven demons before He met her. She would not fit anyone's profile for the kind of friend we all want to have.

She was desperately broken and needy, yet Jesus extended an offer for friendship.

Zacchaeus

Zacchaeus's story can be found in Luke 19:1–10. When it came to assets, Zacchaeus did have one thing going for him; he was filthy rich (v. 2). But he was a small little man with a nasty habit of robbing other people blind. You know the song. Zacchaeus was a wee little man (and a wee little man was he). Turns out because of his inferior stature and scheming ways, he also had a wee little list of friends.

But Jesus befriended him.

Jesus walked right up to Zacchaeus as he dangled from a sycamore tree and invited Himself over. Zaccheaus gained a new friend and a new outlook on life that day.

What did Jesus gain? Did Zacchaeus write a big fat check to Jesus' ministry? Nope. In fact, he promised to give his wealth back to those he had stolen from and to the poor (v. 8). Jesus didn't gain a penny from this rich new friend. This friendship was not about bankrolling Jesus' big speaking tour.

When looking for potential friends, would you consider small, hated schemers? Nope. Me neither. But Jesus did.

The Adulterous Woman

Let's face it; no one wants to hang out with the stinky kid. We naturally tend to distance ourselves from the social outcast, lest we be outcast with them. But this was not Jesus' SOP.

The story of the adulterous woman found in John 8:1–11 is one of my favorites in all of Scripture. There are layers and layers of lessons to be learned from it. Let me give you a quick summary:

- Jesus is teaching at the temple.
- The scribes and Pharisees bring Him a woman who was literally caught in the act of adultery. (Think public humiliation at its highest form.)
- They want Jesus to give permission for a stoning right then and there because she is such a big-time sinner in their eyes.
- Of course, Jesus isn't down with doing what the Pharisees want Him to do. And while He's all about dealing with our sin, He's also all about grace, so He lovingly stands between the woman and the crowd that desires to stone her to death.

When choosing between the outcast and the in crowd, Jesus chose the outcast. This story isn't the only example of this. He hung out with all manner of undesirables. If you take a hard look at Jesus' relationships in the

Scriptures, it seems that chronic screwups were among His favorite peeps.

Judas

In Luke 6, we find Jesus picking His team. After pulling a prayer all-nighter, He handpicks His disciples. Verse 16 has an interesting little story to tell: ". . . and Judas Iscariot, who became a traitor."

Pay attention. Jesus always knew that Judas would betray Him. He picked him anyway.

There's a fine line to be walked here for sure. There are dangers that come with chronic, toxic relationships. The Bible does warn us that being a companion of fools can hurt us (Prov. 13:20), but we also need to realize that we can't completely insulate ourselves from potential pain in relationships. Our friends will hurt us. Our family will hurt us. That's because they're sinners, not necessarily because we should have never let them into our inner circle.

The Demon-Possessed Man

In Mark 5, Jesus is very intentional about His interaction with a demon-possessed man. Jesus had just finished teaching a large crowd when He asked His disciples to get in a boat with Him. They didn't know where they were going, but Jesus did. He was steering them all toward a radical encounter.

Mark 5:1–2 says, "They came to the other side of the sea, to the country of the Garasenes. And when Jesus had stepped out of the boat, immediately there met him out of the tombs a man with an unclean spirit."

At one point this man had been bound with shackles and chains (v. 4). But no chain could hold him anymore. So, he was banished to live alone among the dead (v. 3). Somewhere along the line, someone had loved him enough to try to restrain him, but that love couldn't hold him anymore. He seemed to be a lost cause.

Verse 5 says that this man could be found wandering the tombs at all hours of the night and day, crying out and cutting himself with rocks.

Does this sound like the kind of person you want to befriend? Me neither. I want friends who are always available to grab sushi and who are willing to give me full access to their chunky jewelry collection. But Jesus didn't keep things so neat and tidy.

Jesus ultimately casts the demons out of this man. There were so many of them, that they called themselves "Legion" (v. 9).

Legion was a source of great agony for the man. Jesus went to the tormented.

Verses 18–19 hit home a powerful point: "As he was getting into the boat, the man who had been possessed with demons begged him that he might be with him. And he did not permit him but said to him, 'Go home to your friends and tell them how much the Lord has done for you, and how he has had mercy on you.'"

Ultimately, part of what Jesus did for the demon-possessed man was to restore His relationships. "Go to your friends," Jesus said. Be reconciled.

Do you go to the tormented? Do you work to restore relationships that have been intensely strained? Yeah. Me neither. Is it possible that we're missing something big?

As I look at Jesus' relationships, I notice several patterns (many of which make me squirm):

- Jesus didn't wait for potential friends to reach out to Him.
- When there was a conflict, He didn't wait for others to come to Him to make things right. He flinched first.
- He didn't pursue friendship because of what was in it for Him.
- He didn't keep score.

Polishing Up the Golden Rule

In Matthew 7, Jesus is teaching important principles about our relationships when He drops this little gem: "So whatever you wish that others would do to you, do also to them, for this is the Law and the Prophets" (v. 12).

We've come to identify this teaching as the Golden Rule. Later in Matthew, Jesus presented this same concept in a slightly different wrapper by saying that loving others as yourself is the second greatest commandment (Matt. 22:39).

These verses urge us to love others in the same way we want to be loved, but they are not a guarantee that the favor will be returned. The Golden Rule is not an invitation to keep score.

When it comes to my relationships, I tend to think thoughts like these:

I was nice to you today, so you better always be nice to me.

I forgave you, but you better not ever hurt me again . . . or else.

I helped you, so you better help me.

But this is not the spirit of the Golden Rule. And let's face it; it doesn't make for great relationships. If we want to know and be known we need to stop keeping score. If we want to move toward worrying less about having the right friends and put effort toward loving like Jesus did, we've got to learn to love others well without constantly wondering, *What's in this for me?*

When Jesus gives us the second greatest commandment, what is He really commanding?

John Piper puts it this way, "He is commanding that our self-love, which has now discovered its fulfillment in God-love, be the measure and the con-

> If we want to know
> and be known
> we need to stop
> keeping score.
> #connected

tent of our neighbor-love. Or, to put it another way, he is commanding that our inborn self-seeking, which has now been transposed into God-seeking, overflow and extend itself to our neighbor."[1]

Others' Esteem

Jesus doesn't ask us to love others extravagantly simply so the neighborhood can hold hands and sing "Kumbaya." It's not about warm fuzzies. It's about giving teeth to our faith. It's about letting the abundant love God has demonstrated toward us overflow and impact others instead of keeping it bottled up and to ourselves.

When it comes to our relationships, this is a mark that so many of us miss.

In a culture completely obsessed with feeling good, we've been raised with the idea that our self-esteem should be fed into. We look to our relationships to satisfy our craving for constant ego strokes. This is not the formula that Jesus modeled or taught.

Paul is urging Christians in Philippi to be encouraged by Christ's example when he pens these words: "Do nothing from selfish ambition or conceit, but in humility count others more significant than yourselves" (Phil. 2:3).

Perhaps it's time we outgrow the notion that the purpose of our relationships is to provide a steady drip of feel-good fuel for our delicate self-esteem.

I know what you're thinking . . .

Um . . . I thought this was a book about how to get boatloads of fabulous friends.

I hate to pop your bubble, sister, but that bubble is keeping you cut off from the world. As I've wrestled with loneliness, I've learned that there's more on the line than simply having great friends. If we can feel desperately lonely as wives, daughters, sisters, and friends, the antidote must be found in the *quality* of our relationships, not the *quantity*. The Bible teaches a paradoxical truth (again). The depth and quality of our relationships hinge on what we give, not what we get.

I don't do math (remember, even knitting involved too many calculations for me), but when we look at Jesus' teachings and examples, it becomes clear why our relationship equations so rarely add up. We tend to plug the factors in this way:

Me + relationships built on my self-esteem = shallow connection

We need a new equation that looks like this:

Me + relationships built on others' esteem = deep connection

Here's a taste of what that might look like:

Ashton was new to the area. Her daughter had a birthday approaching, but Ashton knew she couldn't host a party for their new friends at their house. She needed a yard, and their yard was still just mud from the new construction. Another woman from their church, Karen, had a great yard and offered it to be used for Ashton's daughter's party. Although Ashton felt a little awkward because she didn't know Karen all that well, she accepted the offer and invited everyone to Karen's house for the party. The party was a success, and Ashton and Karen continued to be close friends. Karen would continue to serve Ashton as a mentor for years to come; it had become a life-impacting friendship.

Ashton had a need and Karen willingly met it. When it comes to others' esteem, we don't have to offer something big and dramatic. Karen simply offered her yard and her time. Others' esteem means offering what you have to others. It seems rare to me that our friendships are built on this foundation.

Andrea found deep friendship as a side effect of service. As a young mom in a new town, she first met Ed, age seventy, and his sixty-eight-year-old wife, Clara, when they showed up with a moving crew from church. The first time Andrea saw Clara she was standing on her kitchen countertops cleaning her highest cabinets. Ed was upstairs ripping up carpets. Andrea didn't know it, but Ed was on a liquid diet that day because the next day he was having treatment for prostate cancer. But he still selflessly served a family he had never met. This is others-centric living in action.

"Ed and Clara taught me so much about loving others, serving others, and being community," Andrea said. "There was never a need I had they didn't find a way to help with. Ed taught me to till my garden, Clara taught me how to plant it. They could both work circles around me. Ed taught me how to fix my lawn mower. Clara taught me how to cook corned beef and cabbage.

They watched our kids so I could do ministry with my husband. They just did life with me, like they had always known and loved me and my family."

When thinking about friendships, we wouldn't naturally think to match a young family with small children with an older couple battling prostate cancer. There's no room for dinner dates or beach vacations in that scenario. But maybe Andrea, Ed, and Clara found something better than someone to simply spend time with.

"They made me a better person. Their love changed me," Andrea said. "But here's the deal . . . I wasn't the only one they loved like that. That's how they lived. They served and loved on anyone who would let them. I think we got to be so close because I let them love and serve me the most. Without them, I would have been unfathomably lonely in that town."

Did you catch it? Service fights back when loneliness comes calling. The secret to feeling less alone is not to simply wish for others to come into your world to meet your needs. Instead it is to go into their world and meet theirs.

When Julie heard that her daughter's friend Gen had had a massive brain aneurysm at the age of forty, she decided to offer something more than pity. Gen was unable to move or communicate for over a year but Julie went every Tuesday to visit her. She painted Gen's nails, read the Bible to her, and listened to music while Gen slept. It took over eighteen months before Gen could talk back.

Gen and Julie now enjoy a sweet and mutually beneficial friendship, but for months Julie gave and received nothing, not so much as a head nod in return. (Amazingly, when Gen could communicate, she reported that she remembered Julie's visits even though she was in a coma.)

When thinking of potential friends, would you consider someone in a coma as a good candidate? Probably not. But maybe Jesus would. He had a habit of forming relationships with the down and out, the cast aside, and those who had nothing to offer Him in return. Are we missing out on huge blessings when we don't follow His lead?

"About fourteen months after Gen's aneurysm, my oldest grandson, at age ten, was diagnosed with leukemia," Julie told us. "It was a shock and I went out to help as much as I could but couldn't move to help with the weekly trips to the hospital and long stays. God took care of it all when our daughter's church stepped in and graciously helped through many, many unseen needs. So, I did it for nothing in return but, boy, oh, boy, did God ever bless me in return."

It doesn't always work the way that it did for Julie. Sometimes, we give and the favor is never returned but that doesn't change the gift that can be found in the giving.

Bekah is one of my very best friends. If we were in junior high, I'd offer her the other half of my best friend necklace. Bekah and I have nursed each other through several rounds of pre- and postpartum depression. She was at that table of moms where I first confessed my postpartum struggle. She hung in there with me through the weeks it took for me to feel like my old self. A year later it was her turn. She was pregnant with her second baby and her emotions were all over the map. I held her hand. I prayed for her. I took care of her toddler. Fast-forward another year and I was pregnant again. She wasn't afraid to ask hard questions about my state of mind. When my son was born she moved in for a few days as a safety net in case the baby blues came calling.

There is nothing glamorous or feel-good about pregnancy hormones. There is no ego-stroking happening when we look each other in the eye and say, "I am really sad." Walking with each other through painful times has watered the deep roots of our friendship. We are deeply connected because we have served each other. A lifetime of lunch dates could not cause the same result. Sure, we have fun together too but that doesn't bear much fruit.

True, deep connection, the kind that can keep us tethered and hemmed in, is born from sacrifice, not self-esteem. There's no room for an ATM mentality among the people of God.

If we're going to vaccinate ourselves and others against the pandemic of loneliness, we must love like Jesus loved. We've got to connect with people who have nothing to offer us. We should befriend the undesirable and cast out. We need to look at our relationships and ask what we can give instead of what we can get.

> If we're going to vaccinate ourselves and others against the pandemic of loneliness, we must love like Jesus loved. #connected

Sure . . . living this way can be like pulling the bar on a slot machine. Sometimes we will strike out. But then, our luck will turn and service to others will result in deep and meaningful connection. The only way to get that relationship jackpot is by selflessly serving others and letting the chips fall where they may.

CHAPTER 10

When Loneliness Is Your Teacher

Surely, if Jesus had joined our focus groups for this book, His time of tempting in the wilderness would have come up as we probed for stories about loneliness. Matthew 4 describes an intense season of testing and trial that Jesus endured alone. Go ahead and grab your Bible and brush up on your understanding of the story. When looking through the lens of loneliness, you may find something there you never noticed before.

I always imagined Jesus' forty days of testing as some sort of spiritual intensive. Jesus hung out by the campfire, sang worship songs, and occasionally got into a battle of wits with the Devil. Sounds like good ol' church camp stuff to me. But that's not what the wilderness was about.

Before we head into the wilderness we need to jump back to Matthew 3—"This is my beloved Son, with whom I am well pleased" (Matt. 3:17).

These are the words God the Father spoke just before Jesus was led into the wilderness. Jesus was baptized and the heavens literally opened up. The Spirit of God came down like a dove, and God's voice boomed approval from heaven. Talk about a spiritual high! But in a heartbeat, Jesus was led into the wilderness where He faced forty days of intense trial.

The wilderness is the area that surrounded the Dead Sea. It was thirty-five miles long and fifteen miles wide with almost no drinkable water. Because of this, birds were known to drop out of the sky dead mid-flight if they attempted to cross. The ancient Jews called this spot "The Devastation." Not exactly worship songs by the campfire, if you ask me.

This nickname alone provides tremendous context for the forty days Jesus spent in the wilderness. This wasn't a serene camping trip. It wasn't a personal retreat. Jesus' time in "The Devastation" was a time of anguishing trials. My hunch is that it was also a season of intense loneliness.

Jesus did encounter Satan three times in those forty days. I think I can say with certainty that those interactions didn't ease the loneliness of this season for Jesus. Sometimes encounters with those who know us but aren't on our side are the loneliest encounters of all.

Matthew 4:11 tells us that Jesus was joined at one point by angels sent to minister to Him. All of heaven knew what was at stake. When the lonely season was over, it was the presence of the supernatural that Jesus needed most. Pay attention to that. There's a lesson to be learned.

Jesus' time in the wilderness is the first lonely season we read about from His life, but it was not the last. Some of the women we interviewed for this book described loneliness as a constant state of existence, but most experienced loneliness in seasons. Chronic loneliness doesn't have to be a part of the human condition, but it seems that seasonal loneliness does. That's the cloud, but I believe there is a silver lining.

Hebrews 4:15 reminds us that Jesus is not a God who is unfamiliar with what we go through. This includes seasons of loneliness. He has been there. He has walked a mile in your lonely shoes and as we look at how He walked, loneliness takes on a new role. I've said that much of our loneliness is self-imposed. Jesus is different from us in this way, but if we will study how Jesus responded in seasons of loneliness, loneliness becomes our teacher, showing us how to connect with God and others in the way we were designed.

Loneliness in Times of Transition

Immediately after Jesus' time in the wilderness, my Bible adds this little notation: "Jesus Begins His Ministry." The wilderness was the stopgap between Jesus' years of flying under the cultural radar and His very public ministry. It marked a period of dramatic change for Him.

Loneliness is often a side effect of change.

Kailey told us, "I think change is loneliness. When things are constantly changing, you don't have time to make connections; you can't put effort into relationships and you can't keep them around."

Libby found the transition into parenthood to be a lonely one. Katelyn experienced loneliness after a move. Dianne felt lonely when she started to care for her aging parents.

When life is trucking along at a steady and predictable pace, we tend to go on autopilot. We accept the status quo in our relationships with God and others. Sometimes we need times of transition to shake things up and reenergize us for connection.

Right after Jesus' time in the wilderness, He selected His twelve disciples. Loneliness can be the spark that pushes us to nurture our existing relationships and to make an effort toward finding new ones. It can also motivate us to reach out to our Maker with renewed passion and energy.

In Psalm 142, King David is described as "being in the cave." Most likely David wrote this while he was in the Cave of Adullam where he fled because Saul was determined to kill him. Much like the wilderness was for Jesus, the cave was a stopgap for David. It was where he stayed in between a season as a warrior in Saul's army and his anointing as Saul's successor. No doubt, the cave was a lonely place.

> Loneliness can be the spark that pushes us to nurture our existing relationships and to make an effort toward finding new ones. #connected

It was in that lonely place that David wrote these words:

> Look to the right and see:
> there is none who takes notice of me;
> no refuge remains to me;
> no one cares for my soul.
>
> I cry to you, O LORD;
> I say, "You are my refuge,
> my portion in the land of the living." (vv. 4–5)

"There is none who takes notice of me."

"No one cares for my soul."

These are the laments of loneliness, aren't they? We feel ignored and abandoned, left to fend for ourselves in whatever circumstances create a cave or wilderness around us. But David knew that while his feelings said that he was alone, the truth was that God was right there with him. No matter what season of transition we face, God is ever present. He is a refuge from the gnawing pain of loneliness. He consistently seeks to know and be known in a life filled with inconsistencies.

Lonely Lesson #1: During seasons of lonely change, God is a constant presence.

Loneliness in Times of Sorrow

Katelyn had just moved to a new town when her grandma died after a long battle with cancer. She wasn't close enough to the people in her new environment to bring up her pain. Through tears she described that period as a season of deep loneliness.

Kerrie told a similar tale.

"The loneliest times in my life were times that I was experiencing loss. My mom died when I was in my early twenties and none of my friends had experienced that kind of loss before. I remember a time when I was driving to my new teaching job, my mom had died, and on the radio they were talking about a Thanksgiving meal. I realized that my mom had never taught me how to make the Thanksgiving meal. I just lost it. I remember feeling so alone and in charge of my whole family."

The pain of giving birth to a premature baby pushed Angel into a lonely season.

"I didn't really share what I was feeling or thinking," Angel said of that time. "When people would come to the hospital, it just made me uncomfortable because I didn't feel I could be real. I had to put on a strong face."

When the baby had heart surgery, the elders from Angel's church came to pray with the family but Angel retreated to a room by herself. The pain she was feeling made her uncomfortable and the presence of other people aggravated her uneasiness.

Sorrow has a tendency to box us into a lonely corner.

In Matthew 26 we find Jesus retreated to the Garden of Gethsemane as the weight of the coming crucifixion fell on His shoulders with a thud. He left most of His disciples on the fringe of the garden and took His closest friends—Peter, James, and John—farther in.

Verse 37 tells us that Jesus began to be "sorrowful and troubled." He shared His sorrow with His friends. Remember this is where He said, "My soul is very sorrowful, even to death; remain here, and watch with me" (v. 38).

But they did not watch. They slept. Three times the Bible records that Jesus was so troubled that He fell on His face before the Father. And three times He found His closest friends sleeping instead of supporting Him through prayer. By the time they came around to His needs, it was too late. The soldiers who intended to capture Jesus were within the garden walls.

What would have happened if the disciples had prayed instead of slept? Would the soldiers have been deterred? Would the crucifixion have been avoided? Would Jesus' sorrow over what was about to go down have ended? I don't think so. This incident seems to give us a clear picture of the designed order of our relationships.

When we face a time of sorrow, we want somebody, anybody, to carry us through. When we are worried, or anxious, or sad, we tend to want the comfort of a flesh-and-blood person, but they cannot always give us what we really need.

Jesus lay flat on the ground and cried out to the Father. Like Jesus, when we face times of great sorrow, we need supernatural shoring up.

Lonely Lesson #2: During lonely seasons of sorrow, we need the kind of comfort only God can give.

Loneliness in Seasons of Betrayal

Judas arranged for the soldiers to snatch Jesus in the Garden of Gethsemane in exchange for a bag of silver. Jesus knew that betrayal was coming, but I doubt that made it any easier to experience.

The second round of betrayal was likely even more painful. Peter was one of Jesus' closest friends, a part of an inner, inner circle that Jesus allowed to know Him best. You would think that after dropping the ball so hard in the Garden of Gethsemane, that Peter would get his game face on. But we all know that's not how this story goes. While Jesus was busy being on trial for His life, Peter was busy acting like he never knew Him. There is no doubt that it's lonely when the people you love and trust the most turn tail and run.

I could give you stories of betrayal from our focus groups here, but you don't need them. You've got your own stories to tell. Stories about people who disappointed you, abandoned you, betrayed you, and rejected you. Stories of friendships that turned sour or family relationships that inflicted pain. And if we're honest, we're probably all a lot more like Judas and Peter than we think. We've betrayed others too. Broken relationships are simply part of the bargain this side of heaven.

What lesson can loneliness teach us when we face seasons of betrayal? That forgiveness is required for knowing and being known.

Lonely Lesson #3: Forgiveness is mandatory for connection.

After Jesus' death and resurrection, we see an example of connection at its sweetest in John 21. The disciples were out fishing, likely licking their wounds from all that had just happened. As they rowed their boat to shore they found Jesus, simply cooking them breakfast.

While they ate, Jesus gave Peter the chance to be reconciled. Three times Jesus asked Peter if He loved Him. It's no coincidence that, just days before, Peter had denied Jesus three times. Jesus offered sweet, easy forgiveness and reconciliation. Peter didn't deserve it and he was likely too ashamed to ask for it, but Jesus gave forgiveness anyway. Peter betrayed. Jesus forgave. It's a no-brainer which example we should follow.

Peter betrayed Jesus repeatedly, but his betrayal was not beyond the scope of Jesus' forgiveness. We can take great hope in that truth as we seek to know and be known by the Savior.

Loneliness When There's a Cross to Carry

I think Simon of Cyrene may be one of the most blessed men in all of history.

The Bible sums up his story in one single verse: "And they compelled a passerby, Simon of Cyrene, who was coming in from the country, the father of Alexander and Rufus, to carry his cross" (Mark 15:21).

Simon was an average guy—a father of two who was likely visiting Jerusalem for the Passover when a cross was placed on his back. But this was not just any cross. This was the cross of Christ. This was the greatest instrument of grace the world would ever know. This was the scene of the most important rescue mission there would ever be. This was the place that Jesus would die for Simon's sins. And for Alexander's sins. And for Rufus's sins. And for your sins and for my sins.

Jesus carried that cross for us and for the briefest of moments Simon carried it for Him. But Simon could only go so far. Ultimately, the cross was a burden that only Jesus could bear. That walk up the hill to Golgotha was surely a lonely one, and as Jesus later hung on the cross that Simon carried, He did so alone.

None of us will ever bear a literal cross the way that Jesus did. That fact alone is enough to cause us to rejoice even in lonely valleys, but we do have crosses to bear. There are things that we must carry alone. Whether it's an illness, or a fear, or an experience, or a wound, we all have things that we cannot successfully pass off to someone else to carry. When that happens, we can take courage that we are in good company.

Once on the cross, Jesus repeated a pattern we saw throughout His entire life. He cried out to God the Father: "And at the ninth hour Jesus cried with a loud voice, 'Eloi, Eloi, lema sabachthani?' which means, 'My God, my God, why have you forsaken me?'" (Mark 15:34).

In that lonely season Jesus craved the presence of God. It was what He needed most in His most desperate moment.

Lonely Lesson #4: The antidote to our loneliness is the presence of God.

This is the loneliest moment in all of history. God, who had always been steadfast before and has always been steadfast since, allowed His Son to bear our sins on that cross alone.

Soak that in for a minute. Let it marinate. Jesus bore a season of unthinkable loneliness so that you could be reconciled to the Father. He bore the cross alone so that you could know and be known. He was lonely so that we never have to be. God's presence is the eternal answer to our lonely state.

Class Not Dismissed

When Hollywood decided to tell the story of the cross on the big screen, I joined millions of other viewers by racing to the theater to watch. With a jumbo tub of popcorn in my lap (extra butter, please), I leaned back in my stadium seat as if I was going to be entertained by another blockbuster.

But this was the story of Christ's agonizing death. It was the story of God's great sacrifice. As I saw the images of the bloodied and humiliated Savior, I wondered how I had become so desensitized. I ran out of the theater and did not return. I couldn't bear to watch what Jesus did for me.

The gospel can become so familiar to us that we forget the gravity of it. Life has a strange way of rocking us to sleep so that we miss the big stuff. But we need a wake-up call now and then. We need to remember the truth about who God is and what He has done for us. We need to be reminded that we can have a relationship with God and that He is willing and able to satisfy our deepest cravings to be known. Because of this, the lonely lessons will keep coming. Like an alarm clock set at regular intervals, loneliness

> God's presence is the eternal answer to our lonely state. #connected

163

is the reminder we need to wake up and be aware of who God is and how much we need Him.

Lonely Lesson #5: Loneliness is a gift of grace because it reminds us of Christ's love and sacrifice.

This is not a lesson easily learned or remembered. So, the next time God has you in the school of loneliness, pay close attention to the Teacher. Jesus' life has much to show us about how to respond to loneliness, but it has even more to teach us about the beautiful truth that we are never alone.

CHAPTER 11

The Good News

Whew! That last chapter was heavy. I feel like we need a group outing for some caramel lattes (extra whip, please) to digest it.

If we *were* discussing this book over coffee, this would be my two cents. The fact that Jesus left heaven to come to Earth where He endured painful seasons of loneliness is a beautiful truth. There's just something about solidarity. And I'm grateful for the reminder that Jesus died alone to reconcile me to the Father. There's just something about perspective. But, where's the feel-good stuff? When I'm facing a season of loneliness, I want a warm fuzzy to wrap up in for comfort. The cross of Christ is rough-hewn and not very snuggly.

Don't act like you weren't thinking the same thing. There's no room for a smarty-pants who likes to debate difficult theology, or liars who like to claim they never need to be comforted in my pretend book club.

Do you remember in chapter 1 how I told you that one of the women in our focus groups described loneliness as "knowing that people aren't thinking about me"? When it comes to our loneliness, that's the itch we really want scratched. That's the fear we really want eased. But the painful truth is, people aren't always thinking about us. Even the people who know us intimately cannot keep us in the forefront of their minds at all times. (Nor should we expect them to.)

That's the bad news.

But friend, there is good news. Very, very good news.

Good News of Great Joy

Imagine you're sitting in a church pew, watching the children's Christmas program. Everyone has their pillowcase headpieces and tinsel halos. The shepherds are tending their sheep (except that one who is waving to Grandma and Grandpa in the back pew), when all of a sudden an angel appears.

I hope you've seen enough of these programs to know what comes next. The angel makes a declaration!

"And the angel said to them, 'Fear not, for behold, I bring you *good news of great joy* that will be for all the people. For unto you is born this day in the city of David a Savior, who is Christ the Lord'" (Luke 2:10–11, emphasis mine).

Good news.

Great joy.

These are the aftershocks of Jesus' coming.

While it's true that thinking through the crucifixion is tough for the most stoic of biblical scholars, it's worth pondering because the cross holds the answer to our deepest longings.

Parade Lessons

On a hot August day, the hubs and I packed up our brood for a kid-friendly outing. There was a street fair in our little town followed by a parade. Let's get something straight—hauling three kids down a crowded street for balloon animals and cotton candy in 90-degree heat is not my idea of fun. I would have chosen a less sticky way to spend my Saturday. But I did it for my kids. Because I love them. Because I want to do fun things with them. Because cotton candy and parades is *their* exact definition of fun.

We did the bounce house thing. We bought all kinds of street fair fare. We checked out the craft booths. We were on our way to stake out a great spot along the parade route when my oldest son had a meltdown that went something like this: "YOU SAID I COULD GET A SWORD MADE OUT OF A BALLOON! I WANT ONE NOW! YOU'RE NOT FAIR!!"

Then he went boneless, right there in the middle of the street fair.

I learned a long time ago that life with kids looks less like a Norman Rockwell painting and more like an episode of *Cops* for our family. (Cue "Bad Boys, Bad Boys" theme song.) If I could have hauled that child off to the slammer, I would have.

Later, as I sat in the heat steaming, I started to make a mental list of all I had done for my kids that day. My list was just starting to get impressive when the Holy Spirit interrupted things. If I could write a sitcom script based on that conversation, it might read a little something like this:

Me: "After all I've done for him, he ought to behave."

Holy Spirit: "That's interesting."

Me: "Do I note a hint of sarcasm?" (Note: If you don't think God likes sarcasm, be sure to check out 1 Kings 18:27 and John 9:27.)

Holy Spirit: "It's just that if doing big things resulted in perfect behavior, you'd be perfect, right?"

Me: "Um, this is not about me. This is about my boy with the bad behavior."

Holy Spirit: "You remember the cross, right?"

Me: "Yes. And frankly it makes me squirm."

Holy Spirit: "That was a pretty big thing Jesus did for you. A huge thing. A supernatural thing. It cost Him everything. If the equation works that parents do big things for their kids and the kids spit out perfect behavior in return, you should be perfect, right?"

Me: "Aw. Man."

Holy Spirit: "You do nice things for your son because you love him. He acts out because he's a toddler. And he's hot. And you let him have cotton candy for breakfast. Your love for him and his behavior should not hinge on each other. And guess what . . . Jesus died for you because He loves you. You act out because you're a sinner (and because you sneak Reese's peanut butter cups for breakfast). His love for you and your ability to be perfect do not hinge on each other."

God didn't interrupt my brooding to make me feel like a failure as a parent. He broke in to remind me of His love. Just in case I was tempted to think God's love is so small that it didn't matter, He decided to remind me that His love is so big that He died for me. And while the dying part is hard to chew on, the love that motivated it really hits the spot.

So there it was, the answer to my most burning question: God loves me. He thinks of me. He sees me.

That day at the parade wasn't the only time God has reminded me of these deep and wonderful truths. As I look back I see a pattern of reminders, stuck like Post-it

Notes all over my life with the message that I am on God's mind.

I need to be reminded of God's love a lot. Like daily. Hourly. Minute by minute. You too? We seem to have collective amnesia about God's love because we see ourselves as we truly are and we know that God sees our bratty side. But God's love does not hinge on our good behavior, or our feelings, or love for Him. It is a love that has always been and always will be. It is a love that compels Him to do whatever is necessary to remove the barriers that keep us from Him.

> God's love does not hinge on our good behavior, or our feelings, or love for Him. #connected

That is the good news of great joy.

The God Who Sees

Hagar was the Egyptian servant of Abram's wife Sarai. You can read her story in Genesis 16. I'll give you the Wikipedia version.

Sarai was old and infertile. Her craving for a baby was so intense that she lost her mind for the briefest of moments and asked her husband to sleep with another woman in order to give her a child. Anyone who has seen an episode of *The Jerry Springer Show* could have predicted that this was going to go wrong, but Abe said okay and soon enough Hagar was pregnant with his baby.

As soon as the stick turned pink, the mean girl stuff started. Hagar and Sarai couldn't stand each other and Abram excused himself from the situation. Eventually Hagar ran away into the wilderness.

The story of Hagar's life teaches a profound lesson about loneliness. Her loneliness was deep and urgent. Her circumstances were forced upon her. When things went bad, no one stuck with her. She was abandoned and alone. A pregnant woman sitting by a spring in the desert is a pretty vivid image of loneliness.

But she was never really alone. (Remember, neither are we.)

An angel of the Lord appeared to Hagar and before she could even tell her side of the story, the angel made it clear that God knew what was going on. He had seen this situation develop. He knew her.

"So she called the name of the LORD who spoke to her, 'You are a God of seeing,' for she said, 'Truly here I have seen him who looks after me'" (Gen. 16:13).

One commentary summed up the encounter this way:

[Hagar] perceived by experience his eye was upon her wherever she was, and saw all she did; saw all her transgressions, her contempt of her mistress, and her flight from her; saw her when she was at the fountain, and reproved and recalled her, and sent her back; saw all the workings of her heart, her repentance and sorrow for her sins; looked and smiled upon her, and gave her exceeding great and precious promises: he looked upon her, both with his eye of omniscience and providence, and with his eye of love, and grace, and mercy.[1]

The name for God we see in this passage is *El Roi*—"the God who sees me." Seeing us is part of who He is. He sees me. He sees you. He is thinking about you. He knows even the parts of your life that happen behind closed doors. He is always, always, always looking after you. If He needs to, He can chase you down in lonely deserts or alongside parade routes to remind you that He is with you.

This is just the tip of the iceberg when it comes to the promises of God. Here are some other truths you can grab and hold onto with both hands the next time you feel disconnected:

- God has known you since before you were in your momma's womb. There was never, ever a time that He did not know you. "Before I formed you in the womb I knew you" (Jer. 1:5).

- He keeps such a close eye on your life that the Bible says He keeps records of your worries and your tears in a bottle. "You have kept count of my tossings; put my tears in your bottle. Are they not in your book?" (Ps. 56:8).

- God sings over you. His love is enough to quiet your constant longing to be known. "The LORD your God is in your midst, a mighty one who will save; he will rejoice over you with gladness; he will quiet you by his love; he will exult over you with loud singing" (Zeph. 3:17).

- God calls you His friend. You can never accurately say you are friendless. "I no longer call you servants, because a servant does not know his master's business. Instead, *I have called you friends*, for everything that I learned from my Father I have made known to you" (John 15:15, NIV, emphasis mine).

- He will never change His mind about you. He will never abandon you. He will never be unfaithful. "The steadfast love of the LORD never ceases; his mercies never come to an end; they are new every morning; great is your faithfulness" (Lam. 3:22–23).

"It is the LORD who goes before you. He will be with you; he will not leave you or forsake you. Do not fear or be dismayed" (Deut. 31:8).

Do you feel lonely because no one is thinking about you? The truth is, since before you were even born, God hasn't stopped thinking about you.

> God calls you His friend. You can never accurately say you are friendless. #connected

Do you feel like no one notices just how hard life can be? God keeps a record of every heartbreak.

Do you feel friendless? Betrayed? Walked out on? The God who created everything out of nothing, who always was and always will be, whose name is Faithful and True calls you His friend. His offer always stands.

Walking Away from the Stream

I wept as I wrote those promises. They are beautiful! But I find it hard to make them stick. In one breath I can be so filled up by the precious love God has for me, and in the next breath I can be wallowing in self-pity, right back in the desert of loneliness.

God doesn't seem frustrated by my memory loss. He is faithful to remind me of His love. But every single time He assures me that I am known, I have a choice to make.

Let's revisit Hagar for a moment to see what that choice looks like:

"So she called the name of the LORD who spoke to her, 'You are a God of seeing,' for she said, 'Truly here I have seen him who looks after me.' Therefore the well was called Beer-lahai-roi; it lies between Kadesh and Bered. And Hagar bore Abram a son, and Abram called the name of his son, whom Hagar bore, Ishmael" (Gen. 16:13–15).

After Hagar encountered *El Roi*, she put her chin up and tackled the challenges of her life head-on. She could have made a different choice. She could have stayed by that stream, waiting for a different kind of comfort. Pining for Sarai to come out and be her best friend. Longing for Abram to love her for who she was, not for her ability to give him a son. Begging for people to see what she had gone through and validate her pain. But she chose to let God be enough. It didn't matter if Abram and Sarai ever loved her. It didn't matter if she and her son ever fit in. God saw her. He looked after her. She let that be enough.

A Big Neon Sign

How about you? Go ahead. Think about your own life. Do you see the reminders of God's love He has placed along the way? I'm sure that they're there and if we could borrow a time machine and check out your future, I know that there are even more reminders of God's knowing and loving to come. Each one offers a crossroads. Will you let the promises of God be enough to combat the ache of loneliness, or will you wait by your own lonely stream, hoping for a different kind of comfort?

I'm not saying it's an easy choice or one you can make once and for all, but it's time we get real about what happens when we refuse to let the promises of God soothe our aches and pains. Looking for love, acceptance, and deep knowing anywhere other than God is like pouring water into a leaky bucket. Only God can truly stop the craving. If we will let it, the rough-hewn cross of Christ can be a tremendous source of comfort because it is like a neon sign signaling that we are loved, we are known, we are treasured. He's done all of the heavy lifting required to satisfy our longing to be known.

That is good news indeed.

CHAPTER 12

Let's Have Church

I live in the Midwest, the very buckle of the Bible Belt. There is a church on every street corner. Christianity defines us just like the St. Louis Arch and Cardinal baseball. Maybe that's why a new billboard that popped up along the interstate near my town made front-page news.

It simply said, "Don't Believe in God? You Are Not Alone."

Funded by a local group of atheists, the purpose of the billboard was to build community among those with no faith. I can only assume they were wondering, "Why should Christians get all the potluck suppers?"

The sign struck a chord. It made national news and lit up the blogosphere. What was it about atheists seeking community that seemed so newsworthy? Why would they go to such great lengths to connect and why should it matter anyway?

That billboard has sat like a stone inside of me. My heart has worked like a rock tumbler, turning the image over and over until this gem has emerged.

Those of us who know God and are known by God hold the only key to true connection. There is no duplicate. Our connection with God and others is the secret to reaching a lost and dying world. They want what we have so desperately they are willing to shout it from an interstate billboard.

> Our connection with God and others is the secret to reaching a lost and dying world. #connected

Remembering the Stakes

During the months that I wrote this book, my grandfather hit a patch of bad health. After a lengthy hospital stay he was moved to a rehab center. We all did our best to visit him often, but it wasn't enough. He had too many days in his room alone. The stretches were too long between visits. He began a rapid and devastating downward spiral.

First, he lost control of most of his bodily functions. He was no longer able to feed himself, drink without assistance, or go to the bathroom on his own. Then, the wires in his brain started to cross. He completely forgot some members of our family and often got confused about who was who. Doctors couldn't explain his decline in health, and we all started to worry that the end was near. We prepared ourselves for the worst. Then a blessed thing happened. Due to insurance red tape, my grandfather couldn't stay at rehab. We had to find a different place for him to live.

We brought him home and arranged for around-the-clock care. The constant presence of another human being had a miraculous effect on him. He started to eat and drink again. He could go to the bathroom unassisted. His mind cleared up. He perked up. The sparkle returned to his eyes. The spring was back in his step.

Just as doctors couldn't explain his sharp decline a few months earlier, they had no explanation for his sudden recovery. My only medical training comes from WebMD. (Be sure to go there if you want to be convinced you have a rare, incurable disease.) I'm certainly not an expert, but my research on the subject of loneliness clued me in to what was happening. Pop got sick because he was lonely. He got well because he was connected.

It's a reality I've started to notice all over the place.

I have two friends who have been diagnosed with cancer this past year. Carrie is a strong believer. She has a church home and she calls the people who attend there her family. From the moment of her diagnosis, she has been transparent about her struggles. She resisted the urge to let pride slap a smiley face on her and readily admitted when she was scared, tired, or hurting. Her road has not been an easy one, but she has not walked it alone. Her cancer is in remission. Carrie told me that cancer has been a tool God used to teach her to be real. She said she learned that truth in a deeper way than she had previously known in thirty-five-plus years of walking with Christ.

Lindsey has cancer too. Her faith is on-again, off-again. She used to go to church, but she found that forming relationships there required too much effort. She warmed a pew for months and eventually stopped going. Lindsey is a widow. Her relationships with her children are strained. When her friendships start to get deep she has a habit of jumping ship. When Lindsey was diagnosed she retreated and became reclusive. She increasingly depends on Facebook to connect. She gushes about her sickness there, but when she is around actual people, she clams up. In person, she doesn't say that she's afraid. She doesn't ask for help when she's hurting. Her prognosis isn't good.

I'm not saying that connection is the cure for cancer, but it doesn't seem to hurt. I don't know if it's truer that sickness is caused by loneliness or that connection is a cure, but I do know that when it comes to loneliness we all need a big, fat wake-up call. Where will we end up if we continue down the path of disconnectedness? What will happen if we keep the secret that we are all feeling alone together?

Who Is Fighting Back?

A group of passionate folks decide to mobilize in a seaside town in England. They organized a service with speakers, readings, and singing. Two hundred and forty people showed up for the first meeting.

Who led the charge? Who passionately spoke from the platform? Was it a church planter? No. A missionary maybe? Wrong again.

The service was led by an atheist and it was part of a rapidly spreading movement. Atheists and agnostics around the globe are forming congregations. They're meeting in pubs and community buildings. They're forming nonreligious rituals for life's big events. Groups are forming at a rapid pace in nearly every pocket of the globe. Organized atheism is catching on.

"People who go to church are healthier, wealthier, live longer and are happier," said Sanderson Jones. Sanderson leads the Sunday Assembly, a community of faithless congregants he started in London. "One of the best things about church is that it is a safe place for everyone and appeals to people with families as well."[1]

Although health, wealth, and longevity are certainly not guaranteed, it's true that church has the power to dramatically improve our lives. But it's not the building that does it. It's not simply the ritual of meeting with others. Church isn't just something we do. Church is the artery that pumps blood to so much that is necessary to run the race of faith well. Church connects us because it is a thread that tethers us to the God who sees us.

When I see billboards screaming that atheists can connect too, or watch as a movement to connect those without faith spreads across the globe, one truth is clear to me: the world desperately wants what we have.

The Bible tells us that the way the lost will recognize our faith in Jesus Christ is that we will have love for one another (John 13:35). We love each other because we know each other. If the world is going to continue to recognize Jesus in us and through us, we can't settle for disconnectedness.

But surely, those without faith are capable of connection? Can't they find another common ground on which to build the foundation of knowing and loving?

> If the world is going to continue to recognize Jesus in us and through us, we can't settle for disconnectedness. #connected

"We love because he first loved us" (1 John 4:19).

We don't know how to love without Him. True, deep connection can only be found through Him. No imposter will ever satisfy. Nothing less will ever do.

Koinonia

In Acts 2, we find a progress report of the very first church. Jesus had been crucified, buried, resurrected, and had returned to the Father. The Holy Spirit came on the day of Pentecost, and God's people got busy with the business of spreading the Good News.

A church was formed in Jerusalem. It quickly spread from there. These early believers didn't know about women's Bible studies and backyard Bible clubs. Church likely wasn't yet a place for children's activities or youth group lock-ins. The focus of the early church was simpler than our modern version: "And they devoted themselves to the apostles' teaching and the fellowship, to the breaking of bread and the prayers" (Acts 2:42).

The mission of the first church was fourfold:

1. Study the apostles' teaching. Our modern version of that is to study the Word.
2. Fellowship.

3. Breaking of bread. We call this communion. It is the act of remembering what Christ did on the cross.
4. Prayer.

One of these things is not like the other.

Study the Bible. Check. We all recognize that as an essential part of living the Christian life. Communion. Uh-huh. I'm with ya. Prayer. Yes. We do that in church and we should. Fellowship? (Cue record scratch sound effect.)

The early Christians recognized that connecting with each other was as essential to the Christian life as prayer, repentance, and good teaching. Sure, we still fellowship, but we seem to be missing something that the early church did not.

Let's take a quick tour of the fellowship halls in the churches I've known.

The fellowship hall in my childhood church had carpet halfway up the walls. There were accordion dividers that could separate one big room into several smaller rooms. They were an aesthetic nightmare. The tile was speckled and dated. There was a smell that reminded me of play dough and spaghetti at the same time. I would not describe the room as warm or inviting.

The church where my husband was on staff must have had the same decorator. The theme was clearly brown, as the floor was brown, the walls were brown, the Formica kitchen counter was brown and the long tables we all sat around on folding chairs were also brown. This room seemed to move away from the vibe of uninviting and into the realm of sterile.

The fellowship hall in our current church doubles as a gym. There are big white walls, hoops on each end, and free throw lines painted on the floor. It's cavernous and impersonal.

I'm not trying to dog on church decorating committees, but I think our fellowship halls provide a good visual for the state of our fellowship. True fellowship is not a place that we go or an event that we plan. Our efforts to squeeze fellowship into a time slot or a room in a building have left us all with deep cravings. The fellowship of believers can be so much more. It has the power to change us and the world around us.

The fellowship mentioned in Acts is really the Greek word *koinonia*. It means to hold something in common. More accurately, it means to hold *everything* in common—every blessing, burden, privilege, or responsibility. It is transparency at its best. Knowing at its sweetest. Fellowship equals relationships. Fellowship does not equal activity.

"God is faithful, by whom you were called into the fellowship of his Son, Jesus Christ our Lord" (1 Cor. 1:9).

"That which we have seen and heard we proclaim also to you, so that you too may have fellowship with us; and indeed our fellowship is with the Father and with his Son Jesus Christ" (1 John 1:3).

We have fellowship because we first have a relationship with Christ. He is the table that we all gather around. He is the cord that connects us.

> We have fellowship because we first have a relationship with Christ. He is the table that we all gather around. #connected

True, deep connection is the unique gift of Christ's followers. But any first grade Sunday school student will tell you we're not supposed to hide it under a bushel. No! We're called to let it shine.

Fellowship is the indispensable means of accomplishing the God-given purpose of the church. The world craves connection to God. Because they do not know Him, they have no idea how to connect with each other.

So Let's Have Church

My kids and I recently accompanied Jason on a business trip. He worked long hours all day and we whittled away our time in a cabin in the boonies. I was starting to really crave human connection, so the whole family headed into the college town nearby to have dinner at a local Irish pub rumored to have killer fish and chips.

When we entered, we saw a sign that said this was a "public house." In the spirit of public houses, there were large tables everywhere and we were encouraged to pull up a chair with folks we did not know and make new friends. My stomach got a knot in it. Sitting with people I did not know in a town where I did not live felt scary to me.

So, I snagged a table only slightly bigger than our family and worked hard at avoiding eye contact with any would-be joiners.

The restaurant had a toy box for the kids and an area for them to play. My littles didn't share my social anxiety and they began playing trucks and airplanes with kids they did not know. They laughed and squealed and forgot they were hungry in the face of new friendship.

I smiled politely at the kids' parents, but my hubs did all of the talking. He doesn't know a stranger.

After our food came, Jason invited a couple that couldn't find a table to join us. I stared at my fish and chips and pretended to be overly busy helping the kids experience tartar sauce. But Jason made small talk, which turned to big talk about families, faith, and ministry.

Before the last fry was eaten, we had made new friends whose company I truly enjoyed. And for the briefest of moments, the loneliness that has been so tough for me to shake, thawed a bit. I felt connected. I felt known.

Looking back, I can see that we didn't just have dinner that night. In a pub in Indiana, we had church.

German Pastor Dietrich Bonhoeffer once said, "Wherever a people prays, there is church; and where the church is, there is never loneliness."[2]

You are a part of the church. I am a part of the church. God's Word gives us everything we need to vaccinate ourselves against loneliness, but we're not supposed to hoard the remedy.

You are not alone. God is always with you. You are not ignored. The God who sees is watching. You are not disconnected. You are tethered to God and to His children. You don't have to hide. Your relationships can't go deep until you peel off the mask.

I hope God's truth has filled your cup up to overflowing through this book. He certainly has filled mine. But, remember, we've got a job to do. There's a lonely pandemic spreading out there. People are desperately lonely.

As followers of Christ, we hold the cure.

Let's have church.

A Note from Erin

The day I finished writing this book, my husband called our closest friends and family members and asked them to join us at our favorite pizza joint to celebrate. Thirty people showed up! Thirty beautiful, sweet people with busy schedules and hectic lives that dropped everything to come and pat my back.

As we ate, I was struck by the beauty of getting to celebrate a book about loneliness with so many people who know me and love me. The seismic shift may have cracked my life from top to bottom, but in the chasm I found the secrets to true connection. Because of that, the lonely valley was a gift.

The next day was not so celebratory.

Jason and I were scheduled to meet with doctors for some scary tests for our son Judah, a newborn at the time. I woke up that morning completely smothered by fear, anxiety, sadness, and guilt. The challenges of the day felt impossible for me to bear.

And they were. They were impossible for me to bear. Alone.

At first, I defaulted to old habits. I tried to slap on a happy face, but it simply would not stick. I tried to deny that I was afraid, but the fear was palpable and could not be hidden. I literally tried to hide in my closet, for fear of how foolish I would look if anyone could see me.

But, we worship the God who sees, no? I can't hide from Him. He has a beautiful habit of chasing me down.

It was the Lord who ministered to my heart first that day, but then He reminded me that He has given me His people as an extension of His love. I sent out the bat signal and asked for prayer from my very closest friends. I showed them the raw, gritty gunk that was in my heart. They did not recoil. They pressed in.

That was a hard day, but it was not a lonely day.

When it comes to the school of loneliness, it seems I am still enrolled. I have to learn and relearn hard lessons about transparency, busyness, and true connection. I have to make myself tend to my relationships and force myself to remember that the joy of being known is worth how scary it is.

I can't tell you you'll never be lonely again. I'm afraid it doesn't work that way. But God's Word is the string you need to connect. His people are the balm you need to soothe your aching heart.

So often, loneliness is not something that is forced upon us, but rather a path we choose to walk. While painful, loneliness is the path of least resistance. Connection takes effort. But it is worth fighting for.

May we find each other on the path less traveled. I'll bring the pizza.

A fan,

e

Thanks!

Any other geeks out there who love to read the thank-you page at the end of a book? If you've made it this far, and call yourself a geek like me, that's good enough to earn you a shout-out. So, here it goes. In no certain order, I'd like to thank . . .

You. I thought of the readers of this book often as I wrote. What prompted you to pick up a book on connection? Did the ache of loneliness ease at all as you read? I truly wish I could invite you all over for a bonfire and hayride at my farm. I'm always in need of a new friend to laugh, share life, and drink caramel lattes with. Know that I spent months praying for you. You occupy a big place in my heart and you're welcome at my place any time.

Dree. Dree Hogue is the genius research assistant behind this book. She gathered great data, interviewed gobs of women, and talked me off the ledge more than once. Dree, those of us who know you are incredibly drawn to your warmth and wisdom. Thanks for letting me into your inner circle and for never wanting out of mine.

Our Focus Group Gals. Speaking of Dree, you may have picked up this book because Dree came to your town and picked your brain. Thank you for sharing your stories. They are the heartbeat of this book. We all love the beauty we see behind your masks.

JLyell. Eating strawberry shortcake with you still ranks among my favorite ways to spend time. Thank you for believing in me and for sweetly stewarding my family. It's my sincerest desire to make you proud.

My small group. I love our crazy, chaotic group. It is a great honor to weave my life into yours. My list of favorite people would certainly include: Victoria, Shay, Rita, Dallas, Traci, Ben, Nick, Amber, Amanda, Matt, Jenni, Chad, Tim, Michelle, Cheryl, and Justin. (We use the term *small group* very loosely!)

My Boys. Eli, Noble, and Judah. You're the best and brightest gift God has ever given me. Loving you is easy because you are so wonderful. I will never stop praying for you to make Jesus known.

Jason. Thank you for knowing me so well and loving me anyway. I could never repay you.

Jesus. Thank You for being the God who sees. I can't wait for the day when I shall know You face-to-face.

Appendix:
Connecting with God
and Others

The following questions can be used to help guide personal reflection (Connecting with God) or group discussion (Connecting with Others).

Chapter 1

Connecting with God

1. Have you ever had a "seismic shift" where the foundation of your relationships seemed to crack?

2. Rate the state of your relationships in each of these areas:

   - Sense of connection
   - Dependability
   - Authenticity
   - Consistency

3. What do you think the church can do to foster connection?

Connecting with Others

1. What are the barriers to connection in this group?

2. What are three steps we can take toward deeper connection with each other?

Chapter 2

Connecting with God

1. List the ways you connect with God.

2. Who are you looking to meet your need for connection? Be specific.

3. Who is looking to you to meet their need for connection? Be specific.

Connecting with Others

1. What baggage have you attached to the idea of needing others? How about with the idea of others needing you?

2. Do you need God? How do you demonstrate this in the way that you live?

Chapter 3

Connecting with God

1. Do you have a Jonathan in your life? Someone with whom your soul is knit together?

2. Why do you think we tend to prefer being loved to being known?

3. What past hurts make you guarded against being known?

Connecting with Others

1. What scares you about being known?

2. Ask the group to share any evidence they've seen in each other's lives to avoid being known through remaining guarded, only seeking approval, catering to the crowd, etc.

Chapter 4

Connecting with God

1. Can you think of a time recently when you chose to seek connection through technology and missed an opportunity for more meaningful connection with others?

2. If you decided to break up with your technology for one month, what would be the major hurdles?

Connecting with Others

1. Do you consider yourself addicted to technology?

2. In what specific ways can we encourage each other to seek balance in this area?

Chapter 5

Connecting with God

1. Can you identify with Dawn (isolated after same sex attraction), the teenagers who reached out to Erin (trapped by sexual sin), or Julie (put up walls because of bitterness, anger, and resentment)?

2. Who do you confess your sin to?

3. Do you wear a mask of perfection to church? What would happen if you took it off?

Connecting with Others

1. Have there been seasons in your life when sin led to isolation and loneliness?

2. Do you have sin you'd like to confess to the group? How can we hold you accountable in this area going forward?

Chapter 6

Connecting with God

1. Whose burdens do you bear? Who bears your burdens?

2. Is there a relationship in your life where you need to seek reconciliation?

3. When has God met you intimately in your pain?

Connecting with Others

1. Describe a lonely season in your own life.

2. What scares you most about making peace with messy?

Chapter 7

Connecting with God

1. Does asking for prayer feel embarrassing to you? What other barriers prevent you from asking others to pray for you?

2. Do you have the courage to be imperfect?

3. Is there evidence that you've believed one of the three pride lies?
   - I am autonomous
   - I am self-sufficient
   - I am sovereign

Connecting with Others

1. How can we pray for you? (Remember, get real!)

2. What areas of your life have you been attempting to spackle (make to look perfect)?

Chapter 8

Connecting with God

1. Take a hard look at your family schedule. Is it more conducive to true connection or sacred deprivation?

2. Do you make a habit of . . .
   - Spending time alone?
   - Honoring the Sabbath?

3. What do you need to do to take control of your schedule?

Connecting with Others

1. Are you suffering from sacred deprivation?

2. What prevents you from taking the time to nurture your relationship with Jesus?

Chapter 9

Connecting with God

1. What is your response to the reality that God chose those who were hard to love as friends?

2. In what ways do you tend to keep score in your relationships?

3. Identify two people in your world in need. How can you demonstrate others-centric friendship toward them this week?

Connecting with Others

1. What kinds of friends do you tend to gravitate toward? Do Jesus' friendships convict you in this area?

2. In what specific ways are you challenged by Philippians 2:3?

Chapter 10

Connecting with God

1. Recall a specific season of loneliness. Looking back, can you identify any lessons learned?

2. As you seek to experience deeper connection, do you need to forgive or ask forgiveness? From whom?

Connecting with Others

1. Do you make a habit of running to God when you're lonely or do you tend to run to people to meet that need?

2. How does the gospel impact your definition of loneliness?

Chapter 11

Connecting with God

1. Looking back on your life, can you identify "Post-it Notes" or reminders of God's deep love for you?

2. Are you comforted by the name given to God by Hagar, *El Roi*—"the God who sees me"?

Connecting with Others

1. Review the promises of God on pages 172–173. What can we do as a group to provide practical reminders of these promises to each other?

2. The truth that God knows you, sees you, loves you, and desires a relationship with you is very clear in Scripture. Is that enough for you?

Chapter 12

Connecting with God

1. Are you involved in a local church? Do you find connection there?

2. If not, what possible barriers exist? (If you're stumped, ask the Lord to assist.)

3. Based on what you've learned, how would you re-define the word *fellowship*?

Connecting with Others

1. Do you pursue fellowship as an essential part of the Christian life?

2. What are three big takeaways you've gotten from this book? How will those impact the way you live going forward?

Notes

Chapter 1

1. "Jodie Foster's Golden Globes Speech: Full Transcript," *ABC News*, January 14, 2013, http://abcnews.go.com/blogs/entertainment/2013/01/full-transcript-jodie-fosters-golden-globes-speech.

2. The Free Dictionary, accessed September 10, 2013, http://www.thefreedictionary.com/pandemic.

3. "How the Last Decade Changed American Life," The Barna Group, July 31, 2013, https://www.barna.org/barna-update/culture/624-how-the-last-decade-changed-american-life#.UjEZyeC6_19.

4. John Cacioppo, "John Cacioppo on Loneliness and the Body," Big Think, November 3, 2008, http://bigthink.com/videos/john-cacioppo-on-loneliness-and-the-body.

5. Ibid.

6. Ibid.

7. Ibid.

8. Ibid.

9. Robin Lloyd, "Loneliness Kills, Study Shows," Live Science, March 31, 2006, http://www.livescience.com/697-loneliness-kills-study-shows.html.

10. Hara Estroff Marano, "The Dangers of Loneliness," *Psychology Today*, July 1, 2003, http://www.psychologytoday.com/articles/200308/the-dangers-loneliness.

11. "Psychologists Study Loneliness and Its Effect On Health," *Medical News Today*, August 21, 2007, http://www.medicalnewstoday.com/releases/80114.php.

12. John Cacioppo, "John Cacioppo on Loneliness and the Body."

13. Ibid.

Chapter 2

1. Matthew Henry, *Genesis*, Matthew Henry Commentary on the Whole Bible, accessed September 12, 2013, http://www.biblestudytools.com/commentaries/matthew-henry-complete/genesis/2.html.

2. Ibid.

3. Ibid.

Chapter 3

1. "Whitney Houston," *Wikipedia*, accessed October 1, 2013.

Chapter 4

1. Richard Hartley-Parkinson, "You Can't Hug a Facebook Friend: Young People Spend So Much Time Online 'They Feel as Lonely as the Elderly,'" August 15, 2011, http://www.dailymail.co.uk/sciencetech/article-2026086/Facebook-Young-people-spend-time-online-theyre-lonely-elderly.html.

2. Alice Truong, "For the First Time, Americans Are Consuming More Digital Media than TV," August 5,

2013, http://www.fastcompany.com/3015282/fast-feed/
for-the-first-time-americans-are-consuming-more-digital-
media-than-tv.

3. Paul Miller, "I'm Still Here: Back Online
after a Year without the Internet," May 1, 2013,
http://www.theverge.com/2013/5/1/4279674/
im-still-here-back-online-after-a-year-without-the-internet.

4. Christina Rogers, "Two Hands on the—Phone?
Industry Study Looks at Driver Distraction," *The Wall
Street Journal*, December 5, 2012, http://blogs.wsj.com/
drivers-seat/2012/12/05/two-hands-on-the-smartphone-
industry-study-looks-at-driver-distraction.

5. Ibid.

6. Sandra Bond Chapman, PhD, "Is Your Brain Being
Wired by Technology?" *Center for Brain Health*, October
18, 2012, http://www.brainhealth.utdallas.edu/blog/
is-your-brain-being-wired-by-technology.

7. Hartley-Parkinson, "You Can't Hug a Facebook
Friend."

8. Associated Press, "South Korea Sees 'Digital
Addiction' in 2.5 Million as Young as Three," *Fox
News*, November 28, 2012, http://www.foxnews.com/
tech/2012/11/28/as-smartphones-proliferate-south-ko-
rea-moves-to-stem-digital-addiction-from-age/.

9. Ibid.

10. Ibid.

11. Betsy Isaacson, "Like-a-Hug Jacket Embraces
the Wearer When Facebook Friends Show their Love,"
The Huffington Post, October 15, 2012, http://www.
huffingtonpost.com/2012/10/15/like-a-hug-jacket-em-
brace_n_1942421.html.

12. Hartley-Parkinson, "You Can't Hug a Facebook
Friend."

13. Ibid.

14. Chapman, "Is Your Brain Being Wired by Technology?"

15. "Psych Basics: Dopamine," *Psychology Today*, accessed August 17, 2013, http://www.psychologytoday. com/basics/dopamine.

16. Gary Small, MD, "Brain Bootcamp: Techno Addicts," *Psychology Today*, July 22, 2009, http://www. psychologytoday.com/blog/brain-bootcamp/200907/ techno-addicts.

17. *Wikipedia*, accessed August 17, 2013, http:// en.wikipedia.org/wiki/Opportunity_cost.

Chapter 5

1. Rebecca Hizny Matalavy, "How Do Lions Hunt?" *eHow*, accessed May 22, 2013, http://www.ehow.com/ how-does_4566330_lions-hunt.html.

2. Portia Nelson, *There's a Hole in My Sidewalk: The Romance of Self-Discovery*, http://www.goodreads.com/ work/quotes/536859-there-s-a-hole-in-my-sidewalk-the-romance-of-self-discovery.

3. "What People Experience in Churches," The Barna Group, January 9, 2012, https://www.barna.org/congrega-tions-articles/556-what-people-experience-in-churches.

4. Ibid.

5. Ibid.

Chapter 7

1. Brené Brown, "Brené Brown: The Power of Vulnerability," filmed June 2010, TED video, 20:20. Posted December 2010, http://www.ted.com/talks/ brene_brown_on_vulnerability.html.

2. Ibid.

3. Ibid.

4. Ibid.

5. Ibid.

6. Ibid.

Chapter 8

1. Esther Zuckerman, "80% of Americans Just Don't Stop Working," *The Atlantic Wire*, July 2, 2012, http://www.theatlanticwire.com/national/2012/07/80-americans-just-dont-stop-working/54133.

2. Dave Kraft, "Busyness Is the New Spirituality," *Resurgence*, accessed September 29, 2013, http://theresurgence.com/2010/09/03/busyness-is-the-new-spirituality.

3. Zuckerman, "80% of Americans Just Don't Stop Working."

4. David K. Randall, "Rethinking Sleep," *New York Times*, September 22, 2012.

5. Joshua Becker, "Helpful Guide to Becoming Unbusy," *Becoming Minimalist*, accessed September 29, 2013, http://www.becomingminimalist.com/un-busy.

6. Michael Ireland, "New Study Finds 'Even Pastors Are Too Busy for God,'" *Religion Today*, August, 7, 2007, http://www.religiontoday.com/news/new-study-finds-even-pastors-are-too-busy-for-god-11550311.html.

7. David Briggs, "The Final Four, Travel Teams and Empty Pews: Who Is Winning the Competition between Sports and Religion?" *Huffington Post*, April 3, 2013, http://www.huffingtonpost.com/david-briggs/final-four-travel-teams-and-empty-pews-who-is-winning-the-competition-between-sports-and-religion_b_3006988.html.

8. Bryan D. Caplan, *Selfish Reasons to Have More Kids* (New York: Basic Books, 2011), 32–33.

Chapter 9

1. John Piper, "Love Your Neighbor as Yourself, Part 2," *Desiring God,* May 7, 1995, http://www.desiringgod.org/resource-library/sermons/love-your-neighbor-as-yourself-part-2.

Chapter 11

1. John Gill, "Genesis 16:13," *John Gill's Exposition of the Bible,* accessed October 4, 2013, http://www.bible-studytools.com/commentaries/gills-exposition-of-the-bible/genesis-16-13.html.

Chapter 12

1. Susan Donaldson James, "Sunday Assembly: A Godless Service Coming to a 'Church' Near You," *ABC News,* September 30, 2013, http://abcnews.go.com/m/story?id=20421596&sid=81&ts=true.

2. Eric Metaxas, *Bonhoeffer: Pastor, Martyr, Prophet, Spy* (Nashville: Thomas Nelson, 2010), 71.